HEARTS BURNING WITHIN US

SCRIPTURE
IN THE PARISH, FOR SMALL PRAYER GROUPS
& FOR PRIVATE PRAYER

PETER MALONE MSC

COVENTRY
PRESS

Published in Australia by
Coventry Press
33 Scoresby Road
Bayswater Vic. 3153
Australia

ISBN 9780648145745

Copyright © Peter Malone 2018

All rights reserved. Other than for the purposes and subject to the conditions prescribed under the *Copyright Act*, no part of this publication may be reproduced, stored in a retrieval system, or transmitted in any form or by any means, electronic, mechanical, photocopying, recording or otherwise, without the prior permission of the publisher.

Scripture quotations are from *The Jerusalem Bible* © 1966 by Darton Longman & Todd Ltd and Doubleday and Company Ltd; and from *The Psalms: A New Translation* © The Grail (England). Reprinted by permission of HarperCollins Publishers Ltd.

First published 2018

Cataloguing-in-Publication entry is available from the National Library of Australia http:/catalogue.nla.gov.au/.

Text design by Filmshot Graphics (FSG)
Cover design by Ian James – www.jgd.com.au

Printed in Australia

CONTENTS

Foreword 6

Introduction 8

The themes 11

Advent and Christmas Seasons 14

1. Advent Hope 14
1. The hope of Isaiah
2. Healing in Isaiah
3. The Annunciation
4. Simeon and Anna
5. The Preaching of John the Baptist

Lenten Season 30

1. Repentance 30
1. David: the Psalms
2. David: his sins
3. The Penitent Woman
4. Zacchaeus, the Money Man
5. Resurrection and Forgiveness

2. God's Servant 45
1. God's Gentle Servant
2. God's Struggling Servant
3. God's Disciple Servant
4. God's Suffering Servant
5. A New Legacy

3. Eucharist 59
1. The Covenant Ritual
2. Elijah and his pilgrimage
3. The feeding of the thousands
4. The Bread of Life
5. The Last Supper

Easter Season 74

1. Women of Faith 74
1. Ruth
2. The Syro-Phoenician Woman
3. Martha
4. Mary Magdalene
5. Mary, Mother of Jesus

2. Stories of Faith 89
1. Abraham
2. Isaiah
3. The woman at the well
4. Peter
5. Witnesses to the Resurrection: Mary Magdalene and Thomas

Throughout the Year 104

1. Justice 104
1. Justice and the Prophet Amos
2. Justice and the Sermon on the Mount
3. Labourers in the vineyard
4. Justice and judgment
5. What is good has been explained to you

2. Jesus' Leadership 118
1. Jesus emptied himself of his divinity
2. Jesus came to serve, not to be served
3. The Good Shepherd
4. A new commandment
5. Authentic authority

3. The Integrity of Creation 133
1. Creation
2. Destruction and new creation
3. Praise of creation
4. Jesus and nature
5. Creation and Eucharist

4. The Heart of God 148
1. God sets his heart on us
2. Nearest to the Father's heart
3. God's gentleness of heart
4. The heart of the law
5. The fullness of God

FOREWORD

During Lent in 2013, parishioners of St Thomas the Apostle Parish at Camp Hill in Brisbane participated in a scriptural Lenten program. After Easter, a group of these parishioners asked if they might continue the journey they had begun with the Scriptures, and so began the search for a suitable program. When none was found, the Scripture-in-Parish program *Hearts burning within us* was devised to meet the need. The author of the program, Fr Peter Malone MSC, was asked to prepare a structured resource that would be readily accessible to participants.

The words "Hearts burning within us" come from the gospel account of the two disciples walking with the Risen Jesus on the road to Emmaus and describes their experience as Jesus opened the Scriptures to them that were about himself (Luke 24:13-35). It picks up the two foundational elements of the program: a personal encounter with the Risen Jesus who speaks to us in the Scriptures, and an opening up of the Scriptures so as to better understand what we are reading.

The Hearts burning within us program consists of modules, each comprising five texts of Scripture on a particular theme. The themes reflect the unfolding story of God's plan in the Scriptures, different aspects of Christian life, and the seasons of the liturgical year. Generally, each module would involve five group sessions across consecutive weeks, after which there might be a break for a few weeks before beginning another module.

A session of the program has two parts, each taking around forty-five minutes. The first part uses a simple form of *Lectio Divina*. Here, participants are invited to give themselves over to a chosen text from the Scriptures, opening their minds to what God is saying to them, allowing the Word to find a home in their hearts, leading them to a new understanding of how the Scriptures lead us to Jesus Christ. Praying with the chosen text of Scripture constitutes this first part of the program.

The second part of each *Hearts burning within us* session is a shared study of and reflection upon the same chosen text from the Scriptures. The session guide assists participants to identify key people, words, themes and images in the text; to understand the context in which the text was written and for whom; to recognise connections with other Scriptural texts; and to appreciate the chosen text as God's revelation. Discussion starters and questions prompt the conversation in faith that constitutes this second part.

From the outset, it was intended that *Hearts burning within us* could be used by a group without requiring the presence of a priest or someone who had studied the Scriptures. Where questions arose that could not be answered during a session, these could be referred for answer at a subsequent session that a priest or other suitable person might be invited to attend. In this way, *Hearts burning within us* serves as a simple, accessible and structured program of formation for anyone seeking to encounter Jesus Christ in the Scriptures.

Fr Stephen Hackett MSC
General Secretary
Australian Catholic Bishops Conference

Introduction

Have you ever had an experience while listening to or reading a Scriptural text and it was so powerful, so moving, so enlightening, so potentially prayer-changing that you could echo the heart-burning words of the disciples in their journey to Emmaus? They had encountered Jesus on the road, not recognising him, telling him of their disappointment at what had happened to Jesus. Then, when Jesus opened the Scriptures about himself and disappeared, they were overwhelmed. 'Were not our hearts burning within us as he explained the Scriptures to us on the road?'.

Heartburn in Scriptural prayer, heartburn as we listen to the proclamation of the Word, can be something that is essential to our life of faith, of hope, of love.

There have been many ways to pray with the Scriptures. This book had its origins in a small parish community group who wanted to pray together, to deepen their prayer. They were influenced by the long tradition of *Lectio Divina*, a way of prayer fostered by the Benedictine tradition.

Wikipedia is not necessarily the most accurate source of information or for definitions. But, this time, their succinct words are helpful:

> In Christianity, *Lectio Divina* (Latin for "Divine Reading") is a traditional Benedictine practice of scriptural reading, meditation and prayer intended to promote communion with God and to increase the knowledge of God's Word. It does not treat Scripture as texts to be studied, but as the Living Word.

The hermits in the early Christian centuries had good memories for the Scriptures and had some access to rare texts. It was the same for the Benedictines from the 6th century – many of the monks were copyists of these texts and artists beautifying the pages with illuminated decoration. This meant that a community gathered, sat in silence, listened to the reader and meditated.

As the Middle Ages approached and more texts had been copied, there was a greater availability, texts found in more and more places. Scholars also wrote commentaries. Priests and deacons preached. Biblical scenes had been illustrated in mosaics, frescoes, paintings, statues, sculptural adornment of cathedrals and churches. The stories came to life in stained glass windows.

And then, in the 15th century came the printing press – the first book printed by Guttenberg was the Bible. While there were translations for the new Protestants, the Catholic Church kept to Latin texts, a sad limitation. Eventually, by the 18th century, translations in their own languages became available to Catholic readers.

Reading the Scriptures tended to be literal. With advances in the study of the languages of biblical times, appreciation of the different ways of storytelling in the past, Protestants first, then, quite some time later, and after a great deal of wariness, Catholics in the 20th century, began to understand the extraordinary richness of the range of literary forms in which God's Word is expressed. Literal, fundamentalist, readings of the Scripture are still prevalent, especially in Evangelical Churches.

While the contemplative tradition of *Lectio Divina* found a renewed strength, members of the clergy and members of religious orders were trained in much more formal structures of meditation points. They found it somewhat straitjacketing but knew no other official ways, having to rely on their own experience or the guidance of wise spiritual directors to break free of the formalities. Meditation could be a dry, disheartening experience.

The Charismatic Renewal and the Jesus movements that gained momentum in the later 1960s opened up different possibilities for prayer, for joyful experiences, for inspiration, gifts of the Spirit. During the 1970s, spiritual directors and retreat guiders encouraged some basic forms of *Lectio Divina*, listening quietly to a Scripture passage, pausing, listening again, sharing a word or phrase that they identified with, finding insight, sometimes a mantra, always a focus – and the possibility for hearts to begin to burn.

It was one of the dreams of the Second Vatican Council that all Catholics would soon become very familiar with the Jewish Scriptures.

While there were more and more students of the Scriptures, it did not quite happen as hoped for. *Lectio Divina* and the recent prayer movements have opened up both Old and New Testaments. The graced history of the Hebrew People - their Law, Torah, their history, their prophets, their wisdom - is now much more accessible.

These writings, prose and poetry, shaped the imaginations of the early Christians and the writing of the Gospels, Acts, Paul's letters and the other letters and the book of Revelation. One of the joys that can light up hearts is hearing the Gospels in the light of the stories, symbols and what we can see now as foreshadowings of Jesus.

And the words and actions of Jesus can become more alive. Readers of Mark's Gospel find it very vivid in its details while Matthew's Gospel is no-frills teaching and the sayings of Jesus. Luke has always been considered a very feeling recounting of Jesus' life and ministry, while the Gospel of John has a mystical, a 'signs and wonders' appeal and fascination.

This series of texts and suggestions for prayer, contemplation and reflection is not presented as something to be followed in any rigid or hard and fast procedure. Rather, the texts chosen, the themes identified, the particular perspectives, especially that of Jesus, the questions for deepening the meaning, are only starting off points. Perhaps they are useful for some discipline and order in moving into prayer. But flexibility is the key. The format is suggestive rather than compulsory!

May you, or your group, or your community, be enriched as you pray, each personally, but – it is hoped – within a common experience of listening to the Scriptures and our hearts burning along the way.

Peter Malone MSC
April 2018

THE THEMES

Introducing the themes

In this book, there are fifty sessions for prayer, for *Lectio Divina* or a variation form of biblical prayer.
    Each session follows the same pattern.

- The text chosen for the *Lectio Divina* prayer.

They have been chosen according to the particular season of the Church's year, both from the Jewish Scriptures and the New Testament. They have been chosen for the various liturgical seasons of the Church's year. The following section How to pray, using the *Lectio Divina* has suggestions about how to use the chosen text.
(Note that the texts are from the Jerusalem Bible (1966), the version currently used at Mass. Unlike more contemporary translations, the Jerusalem Bible uses exclusive language, but it is hoped that the revision of the Lectionary will be more sensitive to the issue of inclusive language.)

- An indication of five themes.

These are listed to indicate something of the scope for the prayer.

- Brief explanation of these themes.

In a sentence or two, the chosen themes for the prayer are opened up.
(Note that in the development of the themes and suggestions for reflection, there are references to sections of the Bible not actually quoted in the chosen passage but part of the larger context of those passages.)

- The scriptural voice for this particular passage, the background for this voice.

This offers the origins of the passage and situates it in the context of the book where it is found.

- Other scriptural voices.

Some indication of passages that are similar to the text that has been chosen and which throw light on it.

- A focus on Jesus himself

We pray to the Father, through Jesus, in the Spirit. There is a Jesus-focus to each text, whether it be from the Jewish scriptures which influenced the writing of the New Testament books, or whether it be from the words and actions of Jesus himself.

- Five suggestions for deepening the meaning of the text and the prayer.

Lectio Divina and biblical prayer assume that our prayer is ever-deepening. Some suggestions are offered for prayerful consideration – and some questions indicate the personal meanings, the communal and community meanings that become our deeper spirituality.

How to pray, using the *Lectio Divina*

[These suggested directions arose within the group at St Thomas the Apostle Parish, Camp Hill, Brisbane, who pioneered the process with the themes. The method is also recommended for personal and private prayer.]

The selected passage of Scripture is read **three or four times,** slowly and thoughtfully, with a silent period of about five minutes after each reading.

On the First Reading, simply listen to the words as these are read aloud. As you listen, note the words or phrases that remain in your awareness. This is a time of personal attentiveness; there is no sharing or discussion.

On the Second Reading, silently reflect on the question, "what in this reading touches my life today?"

This is a time of personal reflection; there is no sharing or discussion.

On the Third Reading, listen anew to the passage, and afterwards ask yourself, "what is God inviting me to do at this moment in my life?" Again, this is a time of personal prayer; there is no sharing or discussion.

On the Fourth Reading, ask nothing; simply be present to the God who is speaking to you in the passage of Scripture and let God's Word speak to your heart. After the fourfold reading of the passage of Scripture, all are invited – but never obliged – to share what they have experienced God's Word saying to them; how the passage has resonated in their life; what they sense God is drawing them to; what has struck them from the passage. This personal sharing may give rise to prayer. This time of sharing and praying ought not to become a group discussion but should remain focused upon God's Word.

ADVENT AND CHRISTMAS SEASONS

1. ADVENT HOPE

1. The Hope of Isaiah

For *Lectio Divina*

A shoot springs from the stock of Jesse,
a scion thrusts from his roots:
on him the spirit of the Lord rests:
a spirit of wisdom and insight,
a spirit of counsel and power,
a spirit of knowledge and of the fear of the Lord...

The wolf lives with the lamb,
the panther lies down with the kid,
calf and lion cub feed together
with a little boy to lead them.
The cow and the bear make friends,
their young lie down together,
The lion eats straw like the ox.
The infant plays over the cobra's hole;
into the viper's lair
the young child puts his hand.
They do no hurt, no harm,
on all my holy mountain,
for the country is filled with the knowledge of the Lord.

Isaiah 11:1-2, 4-9

Themes

The Spirit
Gifts of the Spirit
Creation in harmony
Hope
Peace

Explanation

The Spirit: the Spirit is the breath of God, spoken of in the Genesis creation account, who renews the face of the earth, who enters into the prophets, who is breathed by God into the renewed people.

Gifts of the Spirit: God gives qualities of power, knowledge and love, wisdom and awe to the remnant of faithful people.

Creation in harmony: a return to an Eden-like, new creation with no dangers to human or animal.

Hope: this prophecy looks to a more harmonious future for the faithful people, a hopeful anticipation of what God can do for those who love and live in awe of the Lord.

Peace: the consequence of this harmony is that there will be no hurt, no harm, the knowledge and love of the Lord means complete harmony which is peace.

Voice

This is an oracle from the prophet Isaiah (from c. 740 BC), the statesman-prophet who responded to his vision of God in the Temple with the commitment to speak on God's behalf.

While there is always the challenge to repent, some of Isaiah's oracles have visions of peace – and a symbolic child who will be the true Son of David. This is spelt out in the names of the child, including Prince of Peace (Isaiah 9:5-7). [Many of these texts are incorporated into Handel's *Messiah*.]

Other voices

Throughout the book of Isaiah, there are contributions by many prophets who remain anonymous, who are happy to be part of the book of Isaiah. Chapter 7 offers the image of the maiden and her child (used in Matthew 1), Emmanuel; chapter 8 brings the image of light (used in Matthew 3:16); the first servant song, Isaiah 42:1-12, draws on themes of the spirit, light, conversion and peace. The themes and titles are echoed in Jeremiah 23:5-6.

Jesus

The books of the New Testament were all written in the light of the Jewish Scriptures, drawing on events, characters, symbols to highlight how Jesus can be seen as the fulfilment of the prophecies of Isaiah, the Emmanuel, God with us (Matthew 1:22), the child who is the true Son of David, who is Prince of Peace. These visions of a harmonious life for the faithful remnant foreshadow the reign of God that Jesus announces.

Deepening the meaning

1. Isaiah often speaks of the remnant (a fine description in 4:2). They are the survivors of trouble, those who have repented. God fulfils covenant promises and the prophet offers images of how hopes will be fulfilled. How do we feel as remnant in the difficulties of our lives? Do we believe hopes will be fulfilled?
2. Isaiah contributes to the growing awareness of the Spirit of God, the divine outpouring of life, in creation and in offering a share in God's life by the 'gifts of the Spirit'. How do we understand these gifts of the Spirit and see them active in our lives?
3. The deep human desire for peace can be imaged in many ways. Here it is a new creation where former dangers have disappeared and now there is no harm, no hurt. How relevant are these images of peace today, given disastrous wars and suffering?
4. Peace is a universal desire. Isaiah 2:2-4 had spoken of swords being turned into ploughshares, weapons into tools for service of all. No harm, no hurt is more profound than a child escaping what

used to be dangerous. What is the impact on us of seeing so many children injured in wars or starving in famines?

5. The vision of the future offers hope, the advent of a new age and a new saviour. Have our own experiences encouraged us to be people of vision and hope?

2. Healing in Isaiah

For *Lectio Divina*

The spirit of the Lord has been given to me,
for the Lord has anointed me.
He has sent me to bring good news to the poor,
to bind up hearts that are broken;

to proclaim liberty to captives,
freedom to those in prison;
to proclaim a year of favour from the Lord,
a day of vengeance for our God,

to comfort all those who mourn and to give them
for ashes a garland;
for mourning robe, the oil of gladness,
for despondency, praise.

Isaiah 61:1-3

Themes

Spirit of the Lord
A year of favour
Healing and wholeness
Freedom
Gladness and praise

Explanation

Spirit of the Lord: by now the Spirit that hovered over the waters in creation is seen as God's life poured on specially chosen people, especially the prophets.

A year of favour: see Leviticus 25:9-11, the jubilee year when all debts are cancelled.

Healing and wholeness: the earlier part of the book of Isaiah (Chapter 35:1-10) began to highlight the blind seeing, the deaf hearing and the lame walking as key signs of wholeness and healing when God's special time came.

Freedom: the experience of the people of Israel going into exile in Babylon had a profound effect, signified in the return home and the sense of freedom. Freedom was a special gift of God for those who repented.

Gladness and praise: from now on in Israel's history, there would be no more wars initiated by the leaders. Rather, peace would bring joy in the heart, something that was expressed many times over in the Psalms.

Voice

The text comes from the book of Isaiah, from the third part. The first part - chapters 1-39 – are from the prophet himself and his immediate disciples; the second part - chapters 40-55 – are from the time of the Exile from Jerusalem (587-537 BCE), dramatising the servant of the Lord. The third part consists of chapters 56-66, from a later period, with the joy of the return from exile and a new phase of peace in Israel's history.

Other voices

The vision of healing, freedom and praise begins in the visionary chapters of the early part of Isaiah, chapters 9 and 11, the time of the gifts of the Spirit, of the visionary child of peace, the Prince of Peace. This healing is elaborated more fully in chapter 35:15.

Jesus

This text is read out in the synagogue in Nazareth when Jesus comes back to his home town. Clearly, he is a man of the synagogue, reading 'as he usually did'. But he proclaims that this text is being fulfilled in him even as they listen. The people react hostilely, taking him to the brow of the hill to throw him over. He cannot provide healing and freedom in Nazareth because of their lack of faith. Later, in Luke, he sends the message back with John the Baptist's disciples, that he is the one hoped for because of these very signs (Luke 7:18-24).

Deepening the meaning

1. This text is a key revelation in Luke's Gospel. Jesus is revealed by these signs of healing and freedom. What is the impact on us as we listen to Jesus' stories of healing?
2. The text is an advent text because it offers a vision of hope and joy that a great prophet will fulfil all of God's promises, ultimately, Jesus. Do we experience in our own lives some hope and joy in our expectations? How has God fulfilled promises to us in the past?
3. The year of grace spells out a special time when God intervenes, a hopeful Day of the Lord, when good news of salvation is offered. What are the special gifts of grace that we are longing for at this moment?
4. The theme of the poor, poor in spirit: they experience the handicaps of not seeing, not hearing, not being able to walk, not free. Healing and freedom is the beginning of the coming of the kingdom, of God's reign. How compassionate are we towards the poor and poor of spirit whom we meet every day?
5. This advent role of the prophet is inspired by the very creative spirit of God. Do you see public figure prophets in our times? In what ways are they inspiring?

3. The Annunciation

For *Lectio Divina*

Mary said to the angel, 'But how can this come about, since I am a virgin?' 'The Holy Spirit will come upon you' the angel answered 'and the power of the Most High will cover you with its shadow. And so the child will be holy and will be called Son of God.'

Luke 1:34-35

Themes

Angel Gabriel
Mary of Nazareth
Old Testament allusions
Shadow of the Most High
Son of God

Explanation

Angel Gabriel: it is not just any angel (meaning messenger) to come to Mary, it is Gabriel who was the angel from the book of Daniel (8:16) who announces the fullness of time. Luke says this annunciation is for the fullness of time. Advent waiting is to come to an end.

Mary of Nazareth: Mary is the maiden of Isaiah 7:14 who will give birth to Emmanuel, God-is-with-us. She is the mother who is to give birth (Micah 5:3).

Old Testament allusions: beginning with the reference to Gabriel, this annunciation narrative is filled with allusions to the Old Testament, e.g. an annunciation by an angel to the mother of the judge, Gideon (Judges 6:12), the fulfilment of the coming of the true son of David (2 Samuel 7).

Shadow of the Most High: an expression used to refer to God's power and presence, for example the cloud that goes before the people during the Exodus (13:22, 19:16).

Son of God: while in the Scriptures, all faithful people can be called Son of God (Daughter of God), this reference is to Jesus as the true Son of David, the fulfilment of the promises to David, Son of the Most High, who will rule over the chosen people for ever.

Voice

The infancy narratives of Luke are designed (in the fashion of the traditions of Greek and Roman biographies of great men) to present the subject of the history in the best possible manner. A glance down the side of the *Jerusalem Bible* text shows how many Old Testament references and allusions there are. The Annunciation narrative is like a poetic narrative with all these references.

Other voices

The immediate comparison is with the infancy narratives in Matthew's Gospel where 'fulfilment texts' are offered, especially the explicit reference to Isaiah 7:14 and the virgin being with child. Paul has a reference to the appointed time when God sent his son, born of a woman (Galatians 4:4).

Jesus

Not only is this poetic narrative about the conception of Jesus, it is also an announcing of how he will fulfil the hopes and promises of the Old Testament.

Deepening the meaning

1. An exploration of how Luke weaves the Old Testament references into his narrative opens up the way the early Christian communities appreciated Jesus and his mission. What Old Testament references do you recognise in the Annunciation story? Are there ways of finding out about more of them?

2. Mary is first presented as a modest maiden from Nazareth. Her 'yes' to Gabriel contrasts with the hesitation of Zechariah's response to Gabriel (Luke 1:18). The development of the character and actions of Mary is seen in the immediate narrative of the visitation and the *Magnificat* prayer put into Mary's mouth (1:46-55), echoing the hymn of the barren woman, Hannah, who unexpectedly conceives and gives birth to the prophet, Samuel (1 Samuel 2ff.). Does this awareness of Mary help us understand and appreciate her better?

3. Prophets were called to listen to God's Word and speak it. Mary is pictured as a new prophet, hearing the divine Word, receiving it

and not just speaking it, but incarnating it, and giving birth to the Word. How could we be prophets like Mary, bringing Jesus into our world and the world of others?

4. The *Magnificat* is Mary's prayer, but it is also a prophetic hymn, incorporating prophetic justice themes, about God's final coming and fulfilment of promises. Could the *Magnificat* become one of our daily prayers?

5. While it will be John the Baptist and his preaching that will bring the Advent waiting to an end, with the conception of Jesus through Mary's 'yes', the fulfilment of Advent hopes begins. What happens when we say 'yes' to God, enabling a special presence of God in our lives and the lives of others?

4. Simeon and Anna

For *Lectio Divina*

Now, Master, you can let your servant go in peace,
just as you promised;
because my eyes have seen the salvation
which you have prepared for all the nations to see,
a light to enlighten the pagans
and the glory of your people Israel.

Luke 2:29-32

Themes

The law of the Lord
Simeon and Anna
Comforting of Israel
Fulfilment: Nunc Dimittis
Fulfilment, not without suffering

Explanation

The law of the Lord: Joseph and Mary fulfil the requirements of the law in preparation for Jesus to be the embodiment of God's new law.

Simeon and Anna: they are described as prophets (both a man, Simeon, and a woman, Anna), who are associated with God's presence in the Temple and who, in the prophetic tradition, are filled with the Spirit of God.

Comforting of Israel: In the prophetic tradition, comfort, healing, freedom, are the signs of God's fulfilling the people's longings. In the Latin origins of the word, Comforting is both a soothing and a strengthening.

Fulfilment - Nunc Dimittis: the hymn that is used in the Night Prayer of the Prayer of the Church, the end of the day but the hope of tomorrow, an advent prayer.

Fulfilment, not without suffering: while the advent prayer is full of hope, optimistic about what God promises and achieves, human beings also turn away from God and will cause suffering to Jesus and, symbolically, to his mother.

Voice

This text is part of Luke's infancy narratives (chapters 1 and 2). While it tells (in the tradition of Greek and Roman historians telling the origins of an extraordinary person) the story of Jesus, it also couches its narrative in the tradition of the Old Testament, weaving texts that allude to the history of Israel and God's interventions into the stories.

Other voices

In Matthew's Gospel, Jesus is presented as the new Moses, the new lawgiver who will fulfil Old Testament prophecies. This includes a suffering saviour, a text from Jeremiah 31 about Rachel mourning her children connected with the flight into Egypt and the massacre of the innocents, just as the children of Hebrew mothers were put to death but Moses escaped.

Jesus

Jesus came at the fullness of time, born of a woman (Galatians 4:4) to bring to fulfilment all of the hopes of Israel; the prophecies quoted in Matthew 1 and 2 open up these themes along with the elaborate infancy narratives in Luke 1 and 2 - from a special conception, through his birth, to his childhood, the preparation for his coming to preach the good news of God's reign.

Deepening the meaning

1. Jesus comes to the Temple for fulfilment of the Law. At the Last Supper, John's Gospel will show him to be the new law of love, our love for one another, just like his for us. John's Gospel tells us that when the old temple will be destroyed, it will be raised up, and Jesus himself will be the new temple. Have Simeon and Anna been significant New Testament characters for us?

2. Jesus is designated as a fulfilment of prophecy with two prophets announcing his arrival in the temple, both a male prophet and a female prophet (which is new). Do these rather older prophets remind us of older men and women who inspire us because of their faith and fidelity?

3. In the sermon on the mount, Jesus said that he would not take away one jot from the law, but that it would be fulfilled in him. In his presentation and Mary's purification, the old law's rituals are coming to a close. How important are the laws and rituals of the Church for us? A strong impact? A fading impact?

4. The *Nunc Dimittis* is a key prayer of the church, recited each night by those who are designated to pray the *Prayer of the Church* and by others who want to share in it. As we comfort the elderly, could we pray this prayer with them?

5. According to Luke, Mary, mother of Jesus, was close to Jesus for his first thirty years – and pondered everything in her heart. This included the pain of being the mother of Jesus where this pondering heart was pierced. What is it to ponder in our hearts? Can we find time and space to ponder what has gone on in our lives?

5. The Preaching of John the Baptist

For *Lectio divina*

A feeling of expectancy had grown among the people, who were beginning to think that John might be the Christ, so John declared before them all, 'I baptise you with water, but someone is coming, someone who is more powerful than I am, and I am not fit to undo the strap of his sandals; he will baptise you with the Holy Spirit and fire. His winnowing-fan is in his hand to clear his threshing-floor and to gather the wheat into his barn; but the chaff he will burn in a fire that will never go out'. As well as this, there were many other things he said to exhort the people and to announce the Good News to them.

Luke 3:15-18

Themes

John the Baptist
John the Prophet
Expectancy
Good news
End of advent

Explanation

John the Baptist: his conception and birth are featured in Luke's infancy narratives. They parallel the story of Jesus' birth and conception. Zechariah's hymn, the Benedictus (Luke 1:67-79), recited in the *Prayer of the Church* every day extols John and his coming before Jesus.

John the Prophet: When John is introduced in each Gospel, preaching at the Jordan, he is presented as continuing the function of the Old Testament prophets, announcing God's Word. His manner and style are in the tradition of prophets like Amos.

Expectancy: John creates this atmosphere as preparation for the coming of Jesus, his baptism and the beginning of his public ministry. Crowds who are filled with expectation of something great about to happen come to the Jordan and ask what they must do (Luke 3:10).

Good news: when the crowds ask what they must do after John urges them to repentance, he urges them to sharing, no extortion, no intimidations. They must live their lives with integrity.

End of advent: John is the precursor in the time of hope and expectation of the fulfilment of God's promises. Jesus is to come with the Spirit. Advent is over.

Voice

The text is from Luke and follows his infancy narratives, Luke once again situating these events within the history of the Roman empire. John is referred to as the son of Zechariah (from chapter 1). The tone is the feeling of expectancy (v. 15), that a prophet is among them who demands repentance and integrity of life, that someone greater than John is being announced. And Luke adds immediately that John was arrested and imprisoned by Herod.

Other voices

Matthew, Mark and John all have stories of the preaching of John the Baptist, Matthew and Mark quoting the beginning of the second part of the book of Isaiah (40:3-5) as does Luke. It highlights the continuity between the Old Testament and the New, that John is a prophet to prepare the way of the Lord where all will see the salvation of God.

Jesus

Jesus is announced in this text. Readers of Luke's Gospel will have all the infancy stories in mind (and the broad range of Old Testament quotations and allusions) as John prepares the coming of Jesus. In this context, Jesus will be baptised (his anointing for his ministry) and go on to preach the fullness of the Good News.

Deepening the meaning

1. The verses before the selected text reveal John the Baptist as a true prophet, not pacifying the crowds with false hopes of ease and peace. They must repent, not relying on their ancestry from Abraham as God's chosen people. There must be no presumption. How is John the Baptist's preaching a challenge to our world today? What are the main challenges?
2. John threatens the people with punishment if they do not repent and produce good fruit. To be ready for the coming of salvation, they must find integrity for their lives. How important is repentance in

our lives? Do we acknowledge the wrongs we have done? Do we let ourselves off?

3. One of the key Gospel questions is found in Luke 3:10, 'What then must we do?' John answers this by challenging the people in the practicalities of their daily lives and of the workplace, a perennial challenge. [This question is dramatised in Christopher Koch's The Year of Living Dangerously, both book and film, in the challenge by Billy Kwan.] As we listen to John the Baptist, can we ask in most practical ways, 'what then must I do?'.

4. The pattern of John the Baptist is the pattern for all disciples of Jesus. The spotlight moves away from John; the focus is to be on Jesus. As John says in another Gospel, 'I must grow less and less; he must grow more and more' (John 3:30). When we look at those we admire, well-known religious figures, or those in our closer circle, do we see Jesus growing more and more in them?

5. Expectation and fulfilment: John is the end of the Old Testament, Jesus is the New Testament. Why is John the Baptist held in such high esteem in the Church and over the centuries?

LENTEN SEASON

1. REPENTANCE

1. David: the Psalms

For *Lectio Divina*

Have mercy on me, God, in your kindness.
in your compassion blot out my offence.
O wash me more and more from my guilt
and cleanse me from my sin...

A pure heart create for me, O God,
put a steadfast spirit within me.
do not cast me away from your presence,
nor deprive me of your holy Spirit...

O rescue me, God, my helper,
and my tongue shall sing out your goodness.
O Lord, open my lips
and my tongue shall declare your praise...

my sacrifice, a contrite spirit,
a humbled, contrite heart you will not spurn.

Psalm 51

Themes
Sin
Mercy
Cleanse
Rescue
Pure Heart

Explanation

Sin: also referred to as 'offence'. A personal turning away from God that brings a sense of guilt as God judges.

Mercy: here, God's sense of compassion, forgiveness.

Cleanse: sin and guilt can be washed away which leads to a pure heart.

Rescue: sinners can and must acknowledge guilt but cannot save themselves. This is up to God's reaching out and saving.

Pure heart: the result of forgiveness and cleansing, a heart filled with contrition and with God's spirit.

Voice

While the voice of the speaker/singer of this Psalm has been considered that of David, because of his sinful behaviour with Bathsheba and with Uriah, the voice is that of an anonymous author whose work is attributed to David. The annotation for the Psalm: 'For the choir master... Psalm... Of David...' The prophet Nathan rebuked him because he had been with Bathsheba and this provides the historical context traditionally associated with this Psalm.

Other voices

Isaiah 1:15-18 offers a parallel kind of confession of sinfulness as well as the forgiveness of God: sins like scarlet will be as white as snow. In the prophet Ezekiel, there are three chapters that reflect on individual responsibility for sinfulness, 14:12-23, 18:1-32; 33:10-20. These are the same arguments that Jesus uses in the discussion about the man born blind (John 9).

Jesus

Jesus hears the voice of the contrite heart: the sinful woman in Luke 7:36-50, of Zacchaeus in Luke 19:1-10, of Peter after his denials, of the penitent thief on the cross.

Deepening the meaning

1. Forgiveness comes after a truthful acknowledgment of personal sinfulness - what is evil in your sight I have done - which leads to a humble and contrite heart. How comfortable are we in acknowledging our particular sinfulness? How honest?
2. But the sin is not only something of personal guilt, it has to be acknowledged as an offence against God, who is the judge of the offence, who loves truth in the heart. The Psalmist also says, 'in your light, we see light' – do we see our particular sinfulness in the light of God's truth?
3. Awareness of the offence against God should also mean an awareness of God's compassion and mercy, always ready to forgive. How do we experience God's love, God's forgiveness? How compassionate is our image of God?
4. Forgiveness means an experience of becoming clean again, of being washed clean, for a new life, of not being deprived of God's Spirit. In confessing, acknowledging the truth about ourselves, do we feel cleansed, healed? Experiencing God's life-giving Spirit?
5. After being rescued from sin and being forgiven, the sinner can now rejoice in a pure heart which enables the penitent to praise God and declare God's goodness. Do we ever get stuck in our sinfulness, even in our sense of guilt?

2. David: his sins

For *Lectio Divina*

It happened towards evening when David had risen from his couch and was strolling on the palace roof, that he saw from the roof a woman bathing; the woman was very beautiful. David made inquiries about this woman and was told, "Why, that is Bathsheba, Eliam's daughter, the wife of Uriah the Hittite". Then David sent messengers and had her brought. She came to him, and he slept with her; now she had just purified herself from her courses. She then went home again. The woman conceived and sent word to David, "I am with child".

... David wrote a letter to Joab and sent it by Uriah. In the letter he wrote, "Station Uriah in the thick of the fight then fall back behind him so that he may be struck down and die".

2 Samuel 11:2-5, 14-16

Themes

Coveting
Adultery
Exploitation
Envy
Murder

Explanation

Coveting: David breaks one of the ten commandments. David looks at Bathsheba and covets her, his neighbour's wife.

Adultery: David again breaks one of the ten commandments.

Exploitation: in today's consciousness, we see David as an exploiter and an abuser of a woman.

Envy: the consequences of his adultery and his attitude towards Uriah.

Murder: again, David breaking another of the ten commandments.

Voice

This text is from the Second Book of Samuel. It comes from the 'Deuteronomic History' - the gathering of oral traditions and documents into books after 400 years of the monarchy, from the 7th century BC.

Other voices

2 Samuel 12:1-15 offers a key passage from the Deuteronomic History to make a judgment on David, the prophet Nathan telling him an allegory about a rich man taking the sole lamb of a poor man. David is angry against the rich man. Nathan says, 'You are the man'. Israel never pretended that its leaders were not sinners, even David, so admired as king to whom promises were made that his line would continue forever with the true Son of David.

Jesus

Jesus is seen as a Son of David (lineage through his foster-father, Joseph), David and Bathsheba are both included in the genealogy in Matthew's Gospel, Chapter 1. He is called Son of David by many who call out for his help, like blind Bartimaeus (Mark 10:48).

Deepening the meaning

1. The books of Samuel mostly concern David, including Samuel's choice of him as the king to succeed Saul who was a failure as king. At first, David is presented as an ideal. What has been our impression of David over the years? As ideal? As failure?
2. Unlike other cultures, Israel never pretended that the leaders were perfect. In fact, David is deeply sinful, disobeying the Covenant law. How does awareness of David's sinfulness, even when he was so specially chosen by God, help us to be confident in repenting?
3. But, with the Covenant, God had pledged that he would reach out to the unfaithful people, no matter what. David's sinfulness is grievous but he must be offered the possibility for repentance and forgiveness. David is a model of the Covenant, even in his sinfulness. How aware are we that our God is so forgiving, taking initiatives with us to offer forgiveness?
4. Nathan's short allegory of the rich man and the poor man and the lamb raises David's severe ire. Nathan had voiced God's covenant promises to David. He is the prophet of condemnation and challenge. How hard is it for us to hear that we have done something wrong? To swallow our pride and be honest?

5. David repented – and suffered in atonement: Bathsheba's child dying, and the revolt of his son Absalom. Even with forgiveness, sin has its consequences for the victims and the sinner. Do we understand atonement for what we have done? Not indulging in guilt feelings but taking initiatives to repair what we have damaged?

3. The Penitent Woman

For *Lectio Divina*

... a woman came in, who had a bad name in the town... She waited behind Jesus at his feet, weeping and her tears fell on his feet, and she wiped them away with her hair; then she covered his feet with kisses and anointed them with the ointment...

... She has anointed my feet with ointment. For this reason I tell you that her sins, her many sins, must have been forgiven her, or she would not have shown such great love. It is the one who is forgiven little who shows little love. then he said to her, "Your sins are forgiven". Those who were with him at table began to say to themselves, "Who is this man, that he even forgives sins?" But he said to the woman, "Your faith has saved you; go in peace".

Luke 7:36-50

Themes

Sin
Forgiveness
Love
Peace
Who is this man?

Explanation

Sin: in this context, it is sexual sin on the part of the woman herself but the reality is broader: the collaboration of the woman with the men who exploited her.

Love: before her entry into the house, the woman has been attracted to Jesus, the loving person. She feels love and is emboldened to come to Jesus in repentance.

Forgiveness: not only pardon from sins but, with the consciousness of such sinfulness, the experience of great love enabling the woman to love so much in return.

Peace: the woman has been troubled but, with forgiveness, she is offered tranquillity of heart, and peacefulness in her life.

Who is this man?: this is often interpreted as the dinner guests being indignant at Jesus claiming to forgive sins; another interpretation would have them marvelling at Jesus, that in forgiving he does a God-like thing.

Voice

Luke's Gospel is particularly concerned with women: from Mary, the mother of Jesus, to widows, prostitutes, women on the way to Calvary. This is a sympathetic voice, although rather more harsh on Simon with his pharisaical lack of welcome and courtesy.

Other voices

This story can be seen as a version of The Prodigal Son (Luke 15:11-32) and the forgiveness of Zacchaeus (Luke 19:1-10): loved and forgiven, repenting. There is a parallel with John 8:1-11, the forgiveness of the woman caught in adultery.

The story, in the context of Luke 7 and its parallels with other prophets (like Elijah and the raising of the son of the widow of Nain), draws on the prophet Hosea and his experience with his prostitute wife and his forgiveness for her infidelity.

Jesus

Jesus, we might way, is at his best in dealing with sinners in Luke's Gospel. He is at his most tender and merciful relating to the woman, as he is with the woman caught in adultery in John 8.

Deepening the meaning

1. This is a key story in illustrating Jesus' attitude to sexuality and sinfulness. He says that he knows the woman's sins are many, but they can be forgiven and she can live a new life in peace. In our world, which is often preoccupied with sexuality and with sexual behaviour, how does this Gospel story help us to be compassionate before judging?

2. Simon is affronted by the arrival of the woman who has no place at his dinner. But he is found out insofar as he did not offer the customary welcoming rituals to Jesus. The woman shows more loving courtesy than he has. How righteous are we in condemning others? In not offering them the courtesies of compassion?

3. The story is lavish and extravagant in its use of the alabaster ointment, the woman's kissing Jesus' feet, wiping his feet with her hair – and Jesus' comfortable acceptance of her behaviour, which was wordless but deeply symbolic. There is an emphasis on the sense of touch. How does this detail of the story remind us that God's forgiveness is not like justice given in a court but lavish and abundant?

4. Simon remarks that if Jesus were a prophet he would know the kind of woman who was touching him. For those scripturally alert, there is a parallel between the woman and Gomer, the prostitute wife of the prophet Hosea: his choice of her, the marriage and children, her infidelity and his calling her back in love. How do we see Jesus as compassionate towards those who are judged to have sinned sexually?

5. The cause and effect process is not: 'she loves, therefore she is forgiven', but, rather, 'she is graced and loved so that she can love so much - which leads to repentance and forgiveness'. Do we understand repentance as something of our own initiative or something that is a response to God and grace in our lives?

4. Zacchaeus, the Money Man

For *Lectio Divina*

Zacchaeus... one of the senior tax collectors... ran ahead and climbed a sycamore tree to catch a glimpse of Jesus who was to pass that way. When Jesus reached the spot, he looked up and spoke to him: "Zacchaeus, come down. Hurry, because I must stay at your house today."... They all complained when they saw what was happening. "He has gone to stay at a sinner's house", they said. But Zacchaeus stood his ground and said to the Lord, "Look, sir, I am going to give half of my property to the poor, and if I have cheated anybody I will pay him back four times the amount". And Jesus said to him, "Today salvation is come to this house, because this man too is a son of Abraham; for the Son of Man has come to seek out and save what was lost."

Luke 19:1-10

Themes

Tax collector
Sycamore tree
Complaint
Cheating and repayment
Salvation

Explanation

Tax collector: the tax collectors of the day could be guilty of extortion, greed and fraud. They were despised – and often linked with prostitutes as major sinners.

Sycamore tree: the dramatic way in which Luke tells us that Zacchaeus did something out of the ordinary in recognising Jesus and acted on his interest in Jesus.

Complaint: as with the sinful woman in Luke 7, and at the opening of chapter 15 leading into the parable of the Prodigal Son, the religious leaders profess to be scandalised and complain.

Cheating and repayment: while a sinful prostitute could pour out precious ointment, the tax collector needed restitution in repentance.

Salvation: Zacchaeus is forgiven and can go in peace to a new future.

Voice

Once again, we hear the voice of the compassionate Luke in telling this story of sinfulness, repentance and forgiveness.

Other voices

The main story about a tax collector in each of the first three Gospels is the call of Matthew, the tax collector, who may have collected from the fishermen, Peter and Andrew, James and John. The parable of the Pharisee and the Tax Collector (in Luke 18:9-14) is in the chapter preceding the chapter with Zacchaeus. Zacchaeus' more extraverted prayer of restitution is the same as that of the tax-collector in Luke 18. And it was the prostitutes and tax-collectors who invited Jesus to dine with them which so upset the Pharisees so that Jesus told the story of the prodigal son (Luke 15:1-3).

Jesus

It is Jesus who accepts Zacchaeus' invitation, who calls Matthew, who goes to dine with these sinners and who tells the story critical of the Pharisee and praising the tax collector.

Deepening the meaning

1. While the appeal of Jesus to the prostitutes has a female emphasis, the appeal of Jesus to the tax-collectors has a male emphasis. Jesus is comfortable with men and women, saints and sinners. Why does the story of Zacchaeus appeal to so many people? And used as the Gospel for young children's first reconciliation?

2. In Franco Zeffirelli's film *Jesus of Nazareth,* when Jesus goes to eat with the so-called sinners, he goes to a dinner at Matthew's house and, during the meal, tells the story of the prodigal son. Peter has deliberately stayed away but comes, outside, like the older brother, to listen. At the end, he comes in, weeps and is reconciled with Matthew. Zacchaeus is a financial sinner, indulging in fraud – how easy, or hard, is it to forgive this kind of sinner, especially when we think we are victims?

3. Though they are puns, we can say we can take a leaf out of Zacchaeus' book because he went out on a limb for Jesus and branched out. Are

we a bit more staid than the tree-climbing Zacchaeus in making an effort to reach out to Jesus and forgiveness?

4. Just as the woman kept kneeling at Jesus' feet and kissing them, wiping them with her hair, so Zacchaeus 'stood his ground' and made a public profession of his guilt and of his rectifying all that he had done wrong. Another way of atonement is restitution – have we always been honest in money matters, even small ones – how can we make restitution?

5. Jesus not only proclaims Zacchaeus forgiven but indicates that grace and peace have come to the house of Zacchaeus. Someone lost has been found. Jesus emphasises that he is truly one of the people of Israel, a son of Abraham. How sensitive are we to 'lost sheep' who need finding, especially in our families and our communities?

5. *Resurrection and Forgiveness*

For *Lectio Divina*

The disciples were filled with joy when they saw the Lord, and he said to them again, "Peace be with you.
As the Father sent me,
so am I sending you."

After saying this he breathed on them and said:
> "Receive the Holy Spirit.
> For those who sins you forgive,
> they are forgiven;
> for those who sins you retain,
> they are retained."

John 20:21-23

Themes

Risen Lord
Peace
Holy Spirit
Sins
Forgiveness

Explanation

Risen Lord: The Jesus of Nazareth whom the apostles were used to in their accompaniment of him is now the Lord who has passed through death to a new life.

Peace: after the turbulence and fear that the apostles experienced during the passion, they are re-assured by the risen Lord that they should be calm and in harmony.

Holy Spirit: the creative breath of God, Gift of the Father, now a gift of peace and forgiveness for sinners.

Sins: since the Gospel was finally written by the end of the 1st century AD, the language of sin in John's Gospel comprises personal sin and the sinfulness of the community.

Forgiveness: in the first chapter of John, the Baptist points out Jesus as the Lamb of God who takes away the sins of the world. This has been achieved in Jesus' passion and death. In his love and sacrifice, we can all be pardoned.

Voice

This is one of the key passages from John's Gospel resurrection narrative. The Gospel uses what can be called 'end-language', imaginative language from the Scriptures to express the post-resurrection story of Jesus and the apostles' own experience.

Other voices

There is an echo of Jesus' saying in Matthew 16:19 when Jesus singles out Peter for leadership and speaks of the forgiveness and non-forgiveness of sins. In John 21, Peter himself is forgiven his denials when he affirms his love for Jesus.

Jesus

The Lamb of God who takes away the sins of the world, who preached repentance and God's reign, who forgave sinners during his ministry, communicates this gift of forgiveness to his closest disciples.

Deepening the meaning

1. The first resurrection mission is given to Mary Magdalene, to make known the Risen Lord. She is his first apostle. The peace and forgiveness is the second mission for the Twelve. Both commissions are given on the day of Jesus' resurrection. In Mary's recognition of Jesus and proclaiming her joy, she is a model for us of contemporary evangelisation, making the Good News known – is this in any way part of our living out our life of faith?
2. This is a mission from the risen Jesus who has said 'yes' to the Father in his death, a yes that was accepted by the Father who had sent him to reveal God's reign. How do we understand the Resurrection of Jesus, the completion of Jesus' life and the happiness and heaven of his 'afterlife'?
3. In sending the apostles out and empowering them to forgive, Jesus is doing what the Father did and offering them a Godly mission.

What really is forgiving? Forgiving and forgetting – or something deeper?

4. The Holy Spirit language draws on the Old Testament language of God's Spirit, who was the breath of creation, the gift bestowed on the Servant in the book of Isaiah, the breath that renews the face of the earth – and who is seen descending on Jesus himself. How important is the Holy Spirit in our day-by-day lives, as divine, as inspiring, as encouraging?

5. An interpretation of forgiving and retaining sins is that it is part of the community life, forgiveness is given, but retaining means that there is no forgiveness. How do we deal with those who cannot admit the wrong they have done, who show no sign of repentance? What room is there for patience and compassion?

2. GOD'S SERVANT

1. God's Gentle Servant

For *Lectio Divina*

Here is my servant whom I uphold,
my chosen one in whom my soul delights.
I have endowed him with my spirit
that he may bring true justice to the nations.

He does not cry out or shout aloud,
or make his voice heard in the streets.
He does not break the crushed reed,
nor quench the wavering flame.

Isaiah 42:1-2

Themes

Servant
Delight
Spirit
Justice

Explanation

Servant: while patriarchs like Moses were referred to as God's servants, the word servant took on a new and deeper meaning in this and other texts in the book of Isaiah. The servant is someone chosen and beloved by God who is asked to say 'yes' to a special mission from God. The servant is a gentle disciple who even suffers for others.

Delight: this English word is often used to describe God's attitude towards the people or towards specially chosen servants. The psalm also says, 'God delights in his people' (Psalm 149:4).

Spirit: spirit is an image that refers to the breath and life of a person and can be used to represent the whole person. It is also used for the Spirit of God, the breath of God that creates and sustains the world and renews it.

Justice: at the covenant given by God at Mt Sinai, God is described as just which means, basically, that God is true to the divine self and, therefore, must be true to all people. They then will act justly.

Voice

The prophet who spoke these words is not the prophet Isaiah himself. Rather, he is a later prophet who remains anonymous, but who spoke his oracles in the spirit and language of the prophet and whose words were added to the scrolls named for Isaiah. His words are contained in chapters 40-55.

Other voices

Isaiah 40-55 contains what are called The Servant Songs, which are read liturgically in Holy Week. The *Lectio Divina* passage here is the beginning of the First Song. The others are found in chapter 49, chapter 50 and chapters 52-53.

Jeremiah's call to be a prophet in chapter I of the Book of Jeremiah is God's call to a servant and how the servant would act.

Micah 6:9 urges all people to act justly (referring to the book of the prophet Amos, the prophet of God's and human justice).

Jesus

For Jesus as servant, the baptism narratives have the voice of God quoting this text for Jesus.

For Jesus as servant, the transfiguration narratives also have God using this text for Jesus.

An example of not bruising the crushed reed would be Jesus forgiving the woman taken in adultery (John 8:1-11).

Deepening the meaning

1. How do we understand the meaning of this Servant of God, in his call, in his relationship with God, in what he is asked to do?
2. What is the 'Servant-style' of acting as a messenger from God? In the way of treating people? The Vatican II document on the Church used the image of the Servant, Light of the Nations, for the Church's mission? Do we see this image alive in the Church? Where? In whom?

3. How do we understand this mission in our own times? Who are the crushed reeds and wavering flames in our experience? Are we ourselves? What does this mean in dealing with people in practice?
4. What does justice to the nations mean?
5. What kind of God does this passage reveal? Is this how the God of the Old Testament is generally thought of?

2. GOD'S STRUGGLING SERVANT

For *Lectio Divina*

He said to me, 'You are my servant (Israel)
in whom I shall be glorified';
while I was thinking, 'I have toiled in vain,
I have exhausted myself for nothing';

and all the while my cause was with Yahweh,
my reward with my God.
I was honoured in the eyes of Yahweh,
my God was my strength.

Isaiah 49:3-5

Themes
Servant
Glory
Cause
Yahweh

Explanation

Servant: developing the theme of the servant beloved by God who is gentle in his preaching – the servant now trusts in God and anticipates sharing in God's honour because of his commitment, even though he feels that it has been futile.

Glory: the earliest traditions of Israel describe the grandeur of God as glory. This was manifest in the Exodus story, the glory cloud leading the people in exile, glimpsed on the face of the transfigured Moses, something which God's servants will be given, in which they will share.

Cause: a word used by the prophets Isaiah and Jeremiah with something of desperation. When they think they have failed, they submit themselves completely (their cause) to God.

Yahweh: one of the most reverent names for God, not pronounced by the people of Israel (who said Adonai instead). It comes from Exodus 3, the name 'I am who I am', the living God, spoken to Moses, a guarantee of God's fidelity.

Voice

Again, from Second Isaiah, author of the First Servant Song. The *Lectio Divina* passage is from the Second Servant Song.

Other voices

Jeremiah is the prophet most prone to disappointment and tempted to despair. He prays, I commit my cause to you.

Jesus

Jesus commits his cause to God in the agony in the garden ('not my will but yours be done') and on the cross ('into your hands I commend my spirit').

Jesus is also glorified at the transfiguration in anticipation of the resurrection; and Jesus announces that when he is lifted up, he will be glorified, drawing all people to himself.

At the beginning of the Last Supper, John says it was time for Jesus to be glorified and pass from this world to the Father (his exodus, for the sake of all people to be freed).

Deepening the meaning

1. Consider the feelings of disappointment and frustration of those who are involved in any kind of ministry or service who experience a sense of failure.
2. How hard is it for any preacher or teacher to communicate a sense of what is right?
3. What does it really mean for the prophet, and for ourselves, to say to God, 'I commit my cause to you'?
4. Should a preacher, a teacher or anyone involved in service of others expect acknowledgment and some reward?
5. What does being glorified mean in practice? Glorified by God?

3. God's Disciple Servant

For *Lectio Divina*

Each morning he wakes me to hear,
to listen like a disciple.
The Lord Yahweh has opened my ear.

For my part, I made no resistance,
neither did I turn away.
I offered my back to those who struck me,
my cheeks to those who tore at my beard;
I did not cover my face
against insult and spittle.

The Lord Yahweh comes to my help,
so that I am untouched by the insults.
So, too, I set my face like flint;
I know I shall not be shamed.

Isaiah 50:4-7

Themes

Listening
Disciple
No resistance
Vindication

Explanation

Listening: the role of the prophet and anyone called to minister is, first, to be attentive, to listen to God's Word (which is dynamic, alive and active).

Disciple: one who listens attentively and then puts what is heard into practice, acknowledging the teacher and living the teaching in daily life.

No resistance: initially, the people of Israel were violent, eye for an eye. Slowly, over the centuries, their appreciation of a loving God led to a martyr spirituality, always witnessing to God's love and, sometimes, suffering and dying for it.

Vindication: perhaps not in the worldly court, but certainly in being glorified.

Voice

The third Servant Song, building on the first two. The gentle and beloved servant who commits his cause to God is a true disciple, will suffer for it, but will be glorified.

Other voices

Jeremiah: the prophet of suffering has several stories of persecution (and his puzzlement as to why sinners prospered and the faithful disciples suffer), even to Jeremiah being thrown down a well. He finally goes into exile in Egypt when Jerusalem has been destroyed.

The Psalms, especially Psalm 21, echo this suffering, about the torture of God's faithful.

Jesus

The text for *lectio divina* describes literal suffering: being hit, beard pulled and spat on. The Gospel writers draw on this text for their description of Jesus' passion, especially at the court of Annas, where this brutality and the insults are given as Jesus' suffering in accordance with the prophets.

Before Annas, before Caiaphas and before Pilate, Jesus protests his innocence or is silent. He does not resist the scourging, the crowning with thorns, death on the cross.

The resurrection stories are Jesus' vindication.

Deepening the meaning

1. Authors have written on the cost of discipleship. What does this cost mean? And mean in our lives? What is my/our discipleship day by day?
2. But, the *lectio divina* passage also indicates the delight in waking each morning to listen like a disciple. What is this delight? As we begin each day? As we offer our day to God?
3. Prior to the passage, at the beginning of the Song, the servant sings of being given a disciple's tongue by God. He says it is to know how to reply to the weary, the bruised reeds and the wavering

flames of the first song. Can we see ourselves in the pattern of the Servant? In our listening, in our compassion, in our encouragement of those in need?

4. Should disciples expect persecution? What forms does this take in our part of the world – and beyond – in our 21st century?

5. Who are the best examples of discipleship, persecution and vindication (not necessarily in their lifetime) of recent decades? Who are our role models?

4. God's Suffering Servant

For *Lectio Divina*

... a thing despised and rejected by men,
a man of sorrows and familiar with suffering,
a man to make people screen their faces;
he was despised and we took no account of him.

And yet ours were the sufferings he bore,
ours the sorrows he carried.
But we, we thought of him as someone punished,
struck by God, and brought low.
Yet he was pierced through for our faults,
crushed for our sins.
On him lies a punishment that brings us peace,
and through his wounds we are healed.

Isaiah 53:3-5

Themes

Man of sorrows
Lamb of sacrifice
Sin
Healing

Explanation

Man of sorrows: Adam was originally the man. Several characters are referred to as man, Son of Man. This man of sorrows is the Servant who is now tortured, suffers and dies.

Lamb of sacrifice: the Servant, later in this song, is likened to the lamb led to the slaughterhouse. The image comes of the lamb-victim killed at the time of the Exodus, whose blood was sprinkled on the lintels of the houses of Israel to save the firstborn sons. This theme was taken up in the Passover lamb.

Sin: at this time, the people of Israel did not think so much of individual sins; that was to come later. This sin is the sinfulness of the people in their basic infidelity to the call of the covenant.

Healing: this passage is one of the earliest in the scripture to offer the idea of vicarious suffering: suffering for and on behalf of others. Solidarity in healing and forgiveness after our solidarity in sinfulness.

Voice

This is the final of the Four Servant Songs, building on the fidelity of the Servant, the faithful disciple, and of the persecution, this time even to death. The song does end with some hope,

> His soul's anguish over
> he shall see the light and be content.
> By his sufferings shall my servant justify many,
> taking their faults on himself. (Isaiah 53:13)

At this stage of their history, Israel had no understanding of a life after death (that came in the second century BC), but there is the light of personal fidelity and integrity.

Other voices

As might be expected, Jeremiah echoes the themes of the Servant Songs with his own suffering.

The book of Job is written after the Servant Songs and explores innocent suffering and the mystery of God allowing it (as well as the taunts of his so-called friends).

Over the succeeding decades, the Psalms will take up the theme of suffering, especially throughout the history of Israel (for example, Psalm 105).

Jesus

Pilate says of the scourged and crowned Jesus, 'Behold the Man'. He is the man of sorrows.

The idea of servant was linked in John's Gospel with the image of the lamb. The Baptist identifies Jesus as the Lamb of God.

The Gospels place Jesus' death at the 12th hour, the hour when the lamb for the Passover was killed. On the cross, he is both Servant and Lamb.

The Letter to the Hebrews, chapter 4, speaks of Jesus being tested in every way that we are, though he never sinned.

Deepening the meaning

1. Consider the whole song in the context of Good Friday, where this is the first reading of the liturgy. How does it throw light on Jesus and his suffering and passion?
2. The Song, and the Passion narratives, offer a spirituality of suffering for others – the blend of expiation and reparation (as understood as repairing the destruction that is a consequence of sin). What does this kind of suffering mean in our world, taking on the suffering of others? Why? For what?
3. Re-consider the title, Lamb of God, in the context of the song. How do we see Jesus and his death as imaged by the sacrificial lamb?
4. How do we share in the suffering of Jesus?
5. Commentators are often wary of too strong a focus on Jesus' suffering without enough realisation that the suffering leads to resurrection hope and glory. How does this Servant Song offer risen life hope? When we suffer, do we have resurrection hope, or does it seem to disappear?

5. A New Legacy

For *Lectio Divina*

'Then I am going to take you from among the nations and gather you together from all the foreign countries, and bring you home to your own land. I shall pour clean water over you and you will be cleansed; I shall cleanse you from all your defilement and all your idols. I shall give you a new heart, and put a new spirit in you; I shall remove the heart of stone from your bodies and give you a new heart of flesh instead. I shall put my spirit in you, and make you keep my laws and sincerely respect my observances. You will live in the land I gave your ancestors. You shall be my people and I will be your God.'

Ezekiel 36:24-28

Themes

Water
Heart
Spirit
Covenant

Explanation

Water: water was always a gift for people in a desert country. Water offered refreshment in drink, in cooling, in washing, in cleansing. Water gave life.

Heart: the core of a person, of the whole people (and the heart of God). The heart was the source of life and love but sin could harden the heart and make it cold. New life meant a new heart.

Spirit: the breath of life, creative gift of God in the beginning, bringing the dead back to life.

Covenant: God's pledge of love to the people, a commitment whether the people responded or not. Sin does not break the covenant but draws a renewed gift of forgiveness and love from God.

Voice

The text is from the prophet Ezekiel. His mission was to the people of Israel in the middle of the 6th century BC. Israel had failed the

Covenant and had lost their city of Jerusalem and their temple. They were in exile. Was that the end? Ezekiel and another prophet in the tradition of Isaiah said 'no'. Forgiveness, a new heart, hope, cleansing from sin, the covenant renewed were themes of hope.

Other voices

The prophet Jeremiah (chapter 31:31-34) introduces the theme of the new heart, replacing the heart of stone, the gift of a heart of flesh on which God's law is written.

Genesis I:2, where the Spirit of God hovers over the waters of chaos, the formless void, and creation begins.

Psalm 104:30. Send forth your Spirit and you will renew the face of the earth.

Psalm 42-43: As a doe longs for running streams, so longs my soul for you, my God.

> My soul thirsts for God, the God of my life, when shall I go to see the face of God?

Jesus

John 4: the story of the woman at the well and Jesus offering the gift of living water (himself) which will lead to the Spirit coming into the woman's life.

John 7:37-38. On the last and greatest day of the feast, Jesus stood there and cried out:

> If anyone is thirsty, let them come to me!
> Let them come and drink who believe in me!

As scripture says: from his breast shall flow fountains of living water.

He was speaking of the Spirit which those who believed in him were to receive; for there was no Spirit - as yet Jesus had not yet been glorified.

John 19:33-37: the piercing of Jesus' side and blood and water flowing out.

Deepening the meaning

1. By appreciating the experience of the people of Israel, in the gift of God's covenant love and fidelity and their sin and infidelity, we can appreciate our own lives and our unfaithfulness and need for forgiveness. Looking back over our lives, do we see unfaithfulness? Do we see repentance and forgiveness, for ourselves, for others?
2. We can deepen our image of God and continual faithfulness in reflecting on God's action for Israel as Ezekiel describes in the given text. What understanding of God can we draw from this passage?
3. What do symbols of water, Spirit, heart and covenant pledge of love mean to us?
4. How are these symbols important for our day-by-day spiritual lives?
5. How can they influence our love and work for others?

3. EUCHARIST

1. The Covenant Ritual

For *Lectio Divina*

Moses built an altar at the foot of the mountain, with twelve standing-stones for the twelve tribes of Israel. Then he directed certain young Israelites to offer holocausts and immolate bullocks to the Lord as communion sacrifices. Half of the blood Moses took up and put into basins, the other half he cast on the altar. And taking the Book of the Covenant he read to the listening people, and they said, "We will observe all that the Lord has decreed; we will obey." Then Moses took the blood and cast it towards the people. "This" he said "is the blood of the Covenant that the Lord has made with you, containing all these rules."

Exodus 24:4-8

Themes

Standing-stones
Holocausts
Communion Sacrifices
Book of the Covenant
Blood

Explanation

Standing-stones: using old symbolism, the stones represent the people, the twelve tribes, for this Covenant ritual and ratification.

Holocausts: the animals were completely consumed to show complete surrender to the Lord.

Communion sacrifices: the flesh of the victim was shared by all the people, a sign of the shared blessing of the Covenant.

Book of the Covenant: God's Word was proclaimed for the interpretation of this Covenant ratification.

Blood: for the Hebrew people, the life of all creatures was in the blood.

Voice

Two traditions in the formation of the book of Exodus are intertwined: the 'Yahwistic' tradition emphasising the sacred, the covenant meal in God's presence; and the earthier "Eloistic" tradition with the theme of the sprinkling of the blood.

Other voices

Some precedent for this ritual can be seen in the Passover story, the meal with the lamb, the sprinkling of the blood on the doorposts to save the life of Israel's firstborn (Exodus 11). In the Hebrew tradition, this story merged with the Sinai story to develop the celebration of the Feast of Passover.

Jesus

The Passover is important for Jesus who goes to Jerusalem to celebrate the Last Supper in this context; and see the descriptions of the celebration in each of the Gospels and in 1 Corinthians 11.

Deepening the meaning

1. At Sinai, there is the priest, Aaron, the altar and the sacrifice, sacred readings and the immolation of the victims. How does contemplating the Exodus story of sacrifice and communion offer some deeper meaning for appreciating the Eucharist?
2. There is the language of sacrifice and communion in the Exodus account of the Old Covenant, both significant in the tradition, sacrifice enabling communion. In the celebration of the Mass, how important for us is the reality of Jesus' sacrifice and our communion with him?
3. The twelve stones symbolise the people who listen to God's Word, attend the sacrifice and share in communion. Does the comparison between the sacrifice at Sinai and the Last Supper help us understand the Last Supper better?
4. There is further communion through the sprinkling of the blood - the life-blood - of the victims. The stones are sprinkled as the people symbolically receive the blood and the mountain is sprinkled, the blood touching God, communion with God and one

another through the blood. Does this story help us appreciate better our receiving the host/bread in Communion and in receiving the wine/blood from the chalice?

5. Exodus 24 completes the Covenant chapters: the Covenant itself in chapter 19, the law of the Covenant in chapter 20, the ritual of the Covenant in chapter 24. Can we understand better that Jesus is God's pledge of the new Covenant, his love is the new Covenant Commandment, with the Mass as the ritual of his laying down his life in Love?

2. Elijah and his pilgrimage

For *Lectio Divina*

Elijah himself went on into the wilderness, a day's journey, and sitting under a furze bush he wished he were dead. "Lord," he said "I have had enough. Take my life; I am no better than my ancestors." Then he lay down and went to sleep. But an angel touched him and said, "Get up and eat". He looked round, and there at his head was a scone cooked on hot stones, and a jar of water. He ate and drank and then lay down again. But the angel of the Lord came back a second time and touched him and said, "Get up and eat, or the journey will be too long for you". So he got up and ate and drank, and strengthened by that food he walked for forty days and forty nights until he reached Horeb, the mountain of God.

1 Kings 19:4-8

Themes
Elijah
Angel
Bread and water
Eating and drinking
Strength for the pilgrimage

Explanation

Elijah: one of the major prophets about whom stories were told but who did not write down his oracles. Irascible in his faith, here is a gentler moment for him.

Angel: mediators of God's presence and God's message.

Bread and water: bread the basic nourishment and water the cleanser and life-sustainer.

Eating and drinking: Elijah had already experienced drought when he stayed with the widow of Zarapath (1 Kings 17) who also baked her little supply of flour for scones for the prophet. Now he is offered the same courtesy from God.

Strength for the pilgrimage: Through the angel, God encourages the prophet to gain strength, and make his pilgrimage to God's mountain:

food for the pilgrimage to Horeb, the perfect time, using the symbolic number, forty.

Voice

This is a story, handed down orally, until it was incorporated in the 7th century BC in the books of the history of Israel, the "Deuteronomic History". This story comes from 1 Kings.

Other voices

For further stories of Elijah, they are principally in 1 Kings. He is included in the praise for the ancestors in Sirach 48:1-10 where he is described as rising like a fire.

Jesus

Elijah is mentioned many times in the Gospels where some think John the Baptist is the new Elijah or Elijah returning to earth (because of the description of Elijah leaving earth in a fiery chariot, no mention of his dying). Some think Jesus is Elijah and, during the crucifixion, when Jesus cries out to God ('Eloi'), some think he is calling for Elijah. At the transfiguration, he is seen at Jesus' side representing the prophets as Moses represents the Law.

Deepening the meaning

1. With the reality of bread (and the praise of bread in the Psalms as life-sustaining), we have the origins of the theme of the Bread of Life. How powerful a symbol of life and sustenance is bread in our lives? Do the references in the Psalms and other stories inspire us?

2. God offers bread that is life to revive the despairing prophet who has had enough, wishes he were dead, and asks God to take his life. Do we have similar experiences to those of Elijah, the temptation to give up? What encourages us to hope again?

3. Along with the nourishing bread, Elijah receives water, which will lead to the theme of Living Water. How does God sustain us day by day?

4. God encourages Elijah to come to him, a pilgrimage he can make because of the bread and the water. How is Elijah's experience of God in the gentle breeze and the gift of sustaining bread lived out in our own lives?

5. He has strength for this mission and journey and walks for forty days and forty nights (which is taken up in the story of the temptations of Jesus where the Satan encourages him to turn desert stones into bread and where Jesus in his temptation pilgrimage is sustained for forty days and forty nights). How does the Bread of Life sustain us in our life's journey? How are we encouraged by Jesus' experience and temptations in the desert?

3. The feeding of the thousands

For *Lectio Divina*

Then Jesus took the loaves, gave thanks, and gave them out to all who were sitting ready; he then did the same with the fish, giving out as much as was wanted. When they had eaten enough he said to the disciples, "Pick up the pieces left over, so that nothing gets wasted". So they picked them up, and filled twelve hampers with scraps left over from the meal of five barley loaves. The people, seeing this sign that he had given, said, "This really is the prophet who is to come into the world". Jesus, who could see they were about to come and take him by force and make him king, escaped back to the hills by himself.

John 6:11-15

Themes

Gave thanks
Gave out
Nothing wasted
Sign
Prophet

Explanation

Gave thanks: anticipating the blessing that Jesus would pray at the Last Supper – and with the disciples at Emmaus.

Gave out: Jesus breaks the bread to distribute as he did at the Last Supper and also at Emmaus.

Nothing wasted: Jesus gives in abundance from the loaves and fish. The scraps are collected, value in the leftovers.

Sign: a favourite word in John's Gospel, as in 'signs and wonders'; what may seem an ordinary event is seen as having greater significance and reveals Jesus and his relationship to the Father. The signs and wonders draw us to God.

Prophet: the meal of loaves and fishes reminds the people of the symbolic actions of the prophets, that Jesus is like them, only greater. The people think that he could be their leader and king. But Jesus flees this kind of thinking and interpretation of the sign.

Voice

John's Gospel was written many decades after Jesus' life, death and resurrection. There has been a long oral tradition and the remembered and repeated stories are given new life in a new framework. Jesus is the Son of the Father, revealing him and using devices of signs and wonders stories, like Cana, the woman at the well, the man born blind...

Other voices

Each of the synoptic Gospels has stories of the feeding of the thousands: Matthew 14:13-21; Mark 6:32-44 (and 8:1-10 for the second miracle of the loaves); Luke 9:10-17. The Matthew and Luke versions are straightforward as is the story in Mark except that Mark's version is longer and offers many details of the event.

Jesus

This is Jesus remembered after many decades. This story is recounted as a preamble to the discourse on the Bread of Life. The Old Testament precedent for the multiplication of the loaves comes from 2 Kings 4:42-44.

> A man came from Baal-Shalishah, bringing the man of God bread from the first-fruits, twenty barley loaves and fresh grain in the ear. "Give it to the people to eat", Elisha said. But his servant replied, "How can I serve this to a hundred men?" "Give it to the people to eat" he insisted "for the Lord says this, 'they will eat and have some left over'". He served them; they ate and had some left over, as the Lord had said.

Deepening the meaning

1. Jesus is to be seen in the light of the Old Testament. As the first century went on, the disciples and the Church saw parallels and described Jesus according to the scriptures of the Old Testament. Jesus is a great prophet in that tradition. What is the impact of Jesus feeding the thousands? Do we see ourselves being nourished by Jesus?

2. Elisha's mission was described in the context of an abundance of food from slight origins – "and there was food left over". Do we see - in this image of abundance - God's lavish love for and generosity towards us?

3. Jesus giving the food was in the context of his preaching good news to the disciples who gathered to hear him – the feeding is in the context of opening up the Good News. We speak of food for the mind and heart – how is the Good News, the Gospel, nourishment for our spirit?
4. The chapter is about Jesus as the Bread of Life so the loaves are an important part of this sign as is the multiplication of them and everybody eating. How is this story an image and reminder of how we all share in and are united in the receiving of Jesus' Body and Blood in Communion?
5. Jesus will say to Pilate that he is indeed a king, but not of this world – as he shows here by fleeing from any worldly kingship. Is it a surprise to learn that Jesus escaped after this event, wanting no credit, wanting no acclamation, kingly but not worldly?

4. The Bread of Life

For *Lectio Divina*

"I tell you most solemnly,
you are not looking for me
because you have seen the signs
but because you had all the bread you wanted to eat.
Do not work for food that cannot last,
but work the food that endures to eternal life,
the kind of food the Son of Man is offering you...

Jesus answered: I tell you most solemnly,
it was not Moses who gave you bread from heaven,
it is my Father who gives you the bread from heaven,
the true bread;
for the bread of God
is that which comes down from heaven
and gives life to the world...
"I am the bread of life.
whoever comes to me will never be hungry; whoever believes in me will never thirst."

John 6:26-35

Themes

Food that cannot last
Manna in the desert
I am
Bread of life
Discipleship and faith

Explanation

Food that cannot last: Jesus does not downplay the food that he gave with the multiplication of the loaves – they were just a sign pointing to Jesus himself.

Manna in the desert: In Exodus 16:4, the Israelites in the desert were prone to lose faith in the God who had rescued them from Egypt. In their hunger, God provided nourishment for them which they called Manna.

I am: in John's Gospel, Jesus frequently refers to himself, 'I am', echoing the words of God to Moses at the burning bush (Exodus 3) and giving his name, 'I am' (the living God). Sent by the Father, he says 'I am'.

Bread of life: just as the themes of water and the Spirit of God are combined in the phrase 'Living Water' for cleansing and quenching thirst - spiritual thirst - so Jesus is Living Bread.

Disciples and faith: those who come to Jesus - that is his disciples - will never be hungry again because they have eaten the Bread of Life, and those who have faith will never thirst again because they have drunk Living Water.

Voice

As was noted before, John's Gospel was written many decades after Jesus' life, death and resurrection. There has been a long oral tradition and the remembered and repeated stories are given new life in a new framework of Jesus, son of the Father, revealing him and using devices of signs and wonders stories, like Cana, the woman at the well, the man born blind...

Other voices

The Manna chapter, Exodus 16, narrates the story of some despair and infidelity among the chosen people. The crowd, even after eating the loaves, still ask for a sign. It is they who bring up the Manna story as an Old Covenant sign, 'Our ancestors had manna to eat in the desert, as scripture says, 'He gave them bread from heaven'''.

Jesus

Jesus' final word, as the crowd argue and question how Jesus can give them his flesh to eat, he replies:
>I tell you most solemnly,
>if you do not eat the flesh of the Son of Man
>and drink his blood,
>you will not have life in you.
>Anyone who does eat my flesh and drink my blood
>has eternal life, and I shall raise them up on the last day.
>For my flesh is real food

and my blood is real drink.
whoever eats my flesh and drinks my blood
lives in me
and I live in them.
As I, who am sent by the living Father,
myself draw life from the Father,
so ever whoever eats me will draw life from me.

John 6:52-57

Deepening the meaning

1. Jesus moves from the 'mundane' experience of eating, as in the multiplied loaves, to highlight this as a sign which they must go beyond. Many of Jesus' listeners could not grasp Jesus' meaning. How well do we grasp this for ourselves?
2. We are invited in this chapter to move into symbolic ways of thinking, going beyond ordinary ways of dealing with reality. What are symbolic ways of thinking? Of the spiritual meaning of bread and communion?
3. There is a caution about presumption on God's reaching out to us. God has pledged this and did reach out with Manna to the those in need. But, Jesus, the Bread of Life, is now that guarantee that God will reach out. What is the meaning of the gift of the Manna sustaining God's people in their trials in the desert? A guarantee? How is Jesus, Bread of Life, God's guarantee?
4. Later in chapter 6, those confronting Jesus return to the mundane way of thinking - trapped in literalism – and debate what eating Jesus' flesh means and Jesus answers them clearly in a symbolic, even mystical, way. How well do we understand the meaning of Jesus' presence in the Eucharist? What are the consequences for our faith and our prayer?
5. At the end of chapter 6, when many cannot accept this symbolic way of thinking but are stuck in literalism, Jesus asks Peter and the disciples whether they will continue to follow him. Peter says, 'Lord, to whom shall we go? You have the words of eternal life'. How well can we make Peter's faith-response to Jesus our own response to him?

5. *The Last Supper*

For *Lectio Divina*

For this is what I received from the Lord, and in turn passed on to you: that on the same night that he was betrayed, the Lord Jesus took some bread, and thanked God for it and broke it, and he said, "This is my body, which is for you; do this as a memorial of me". In the same way he took the cup after supper, and said, "This cup is the new covenant in my blood. Whenever you drink it, do this as a memorial of me." Until the Lord comes, therefore, every time you eat this bread and drink this cup, you are proclaiming his death...

1 Corinthians 11:23-27

Themes

Received from the Lord
Pass on to you
Memorial
New Covenant
Proclaim his death

Explanation

Received from the Lord: Paul always links himself and his preaching to the apostolic tradition; he preached the true and authentic tradition.

Pass on to you: Paul's mission is now handing on the tradition to Jewish converts and to pagan converts (and linking the communion to urging his listeners to give up pagan practices).

Memorial: 'Do this in memory of me', not merely a memorial in the sense of reminiscing, but a bringing of the past into the present.

New Covenant: Jesus is the completion of the Old Covenant. He is the New Covenant.

Proclaim his death: the Eucharist, in thanksgiving for the New Covenant, shows what Jesus did in a symbolic-sacramental way, letting the faithful and others alike know what Jesus achieved in his death – and resurrection.

Voice

This description of the Last Supper comes within two decades of Jesus' life and death, from about 54 AD, so it is a description that comes before the writing of the Gospel narratives. Paul speaks of receiving the tradition and of handing it on. The letter was written to the people of Corinth and includes warnings to them to behave well and generously at the celebration.

Other voices

While the Last Supper and 'Institution of the Eucharist' narratives are found in Matthew, Mark and Luke, it is Paul who has a further Eucharistic reflection to the Corinthians:

> The blessing-cup that we bless is a communion with the blood of Christ, and the bread that we break is a communion with the body of Christ. The fact that there is only one loaf means that, though there are many of us, we form a single body because we all have a share in this one loaf.
>
> *1 Corinthians 10:16-17*

Jesus

The Synoptic Gospels offer descriptions of the Last Supper in the context of preparation for the celebration of Passover and of Jesus' words and actions before the sacrificial fulfilment the next day. John's Gospel has chapter 6 focus on Jesus as the Bread of Life and focuses on the washing of the feet and the new commandment of love in the Last Supper chapter 13, followed by the long Last Discourse and the Priestly Prayer, chapter 17.

Deepening the meaning

1. Paul's description of the Last Supper and its meaning indicates how, early in the life of the Church, the disciples were regularly following Jesus' injunction to 'do this in memory of me'. And how the practice had spread from Jerusalem as far as Greece within twenty years. The challenge of our experience of the Mass is our devotion in remembering Jesus.

2. Harking back to the sacrifices, the communion and the sprinkling of the blood which were the features of the Old Covenant in Exodus 24, Paul proclaims - as did Jesus - that these are the signs and pledges of the New Covenant, God's reaching out to the people again in Covenant in Jesus (who is the New Covenant). In contemplating the Exodus stories of the Covenant, what light do they throw on Jesus and the New Covenant?
3. The bread and wine, symbols of sacrifice, realities of communion, are sacred and not to be contaminated by drunken and selfish behaviour in the celebration. How do we find today's celebration of the Mass? Sacred moments? The experience of receiving Communion?
4. Once again, this text of Paul highlights the two aspects of Eucharist. What is our response to the meaning of bread and wine as Body and Blood?
5. While the events of the first Holy Week were 'one-off', they must come to life in the present and, with an eschatological touch, 'until Jesus comes again'. What are the moments of the Last Supper narratives in the Gospels and in Paul to the Corinthians which stay in our hearts?

EASTER SEASON

1. WOMEN OF FAITH

1. Ruth

For *Lectio Divina*

Naomi said to Ruth, 'Look, your sister-in-law has gone back to her people and to her god. You must return too; follow your sister-in-law.' But Ruth said, 'Do not press me to leave you and to turn back from your company, for

> Wherever you go, I will go,
> wherever you live, I will live.
> Your people shall be my people,
> and your God, my God.
> Wherever you die, I will die
> and there I will be buried.
> May Yahweh do this thing to me
> and more also,
> if even death should come between us.

Ruth 1:15-17

Themes

Piety
Loyalty
Faith
Courage

Explanation

Piety: Ruth is a woman from Israel's neighbour, Moab. She was married to a son of Naomi. She was devoted to her husband in love and in sharing his life. She has love and respect for Naomi. This kind of devotion and love in a family and between generations is called piety.

Loyalty: Naomi allows Ruth to stay in Moab rather than come to Israel with her. But in her commitment to her husband, Ruth had made a commitment to her mother-in-law. She opts to go with Naomi rather than stay at home.

Faith: Ruth's piety and loyalty are both personal and religious. She believes in Naomi and in her future with her. She also entrusts herself to Naomi's God and identifies with Naomi's faith.

Courage: Ruth's decision meant leaving behind her land and home and venturing into a completely new life, sight unseen. But, in her new life, she encounters Boaz, marries him, gives birth to Obed and becomes the great-grandmother of King David.

Voice

Ruth's voice is imagined by the tellers of stories from the period when oral narratives were handed down to other storytellers and then to the writers of the books. The books are the witness to God's interventions in the life of Israel. The story of Ruth was also a story of David and all that he meant to Israel – and looking forward to the Son of David, ultimately, Jesus. The name Ruth means Beloved.

Other Voices

Ruth is one of the four women whose names are mentioned in the Prologue to Matthew's Gospel - the genealogy of Jesus: the ill-used Tamar, daughter-in-law of Judah who bore him a son; Rahab, the prostitute who helped Joshua enter Jericho; Bathsheba who became the wife of David; and, finally, Mary the mother of Jesus. The genealogy in Matthew is not a lineage as we would understand it. Rather, there are three sections of fourteen ancestors. The Hebrew letters of David's name add up to fourteen. With three sections, this is a perfect number, so Jesus is a perfect Son of David. The women in the genealogy were seen in the context of sexual irregularity: victim of rape, prostitute, foreign wife to a man of Israel, adulterer. This also highlights Mary's status as an unmarried mother, soon to be elaborated. But the women were victims of men, yet worthy to be ancestors of David. How much more Mary who had consented to God's will?

Jesus

Matthew's Gospel affirms the faith of Ruth, placed in a difficult situation, people from Moab being despised by Israel. In her piety and faith, she is a true Israelite at heart. She is exemplary in her piety and loyalty to her husband, to Naomi and to Boaz, her husband in Israel. Her descendant, Jesus, will share in her humiliations as well in as her devotion and faith.

Deepening the meaning

1. Ruth is one of the rare examples of a woman of faith in the Old Testament. What do we recognise in the main features of her story?
2. The nature of Ruth's faith: not just an assent of her mind or an assertion of belief, but rather a profound commitment to her family and to their God who became her God. How is Ruth's faith an inspiration to us?
3. Ruth's faith and its effect on her life and choices; deep options for a life-choice. Reflecting on the major choices of our lives, deep life-choices, what has inspired us? What has convinced us?
4. How do we connect the consequences of Ruth's faith and a new life with the consequences of faith and courage?
5. Can we see traces of Ruth's faith in the way Jesus is described in the Gospels?

2. The Syro-Phoenician Woman

For *Lectio Divina*

Then out came a Canaanite woman from that district and started shouting, 'Sir, Son of David, take pity on me. My daughter is tormented by a devil'. But he answered her not a word. And his disciples went and pleaded with him. 'Give her what she wants', they said 'because she is shouting after us.' He said in reply, 'I was sent only to the lost sheep of the House of Israel.' But the woman had come up and was kneeling at his feet. 'Lord,' she said 'help me.' He replied, 'It is not fair to take the children's food and throw it to the house-dogs.' She retorted, 'Ah yes, sir; but even house-dogs can eat the scraps that fall from their master's table.' Then Jesus answered her, 'Woman, you have great faith. Let your wish be granted.' And from that moment her daughter was well again.

Matthew 15:21-28

Themes
Concern for others
Hope
Courage
Perseverance

Explanation

Concern for others: the un-named foreign woman, from the territory north of Israel, is concerned not for herself, but for her daughter, tormented by an evil spirit.

Hope: she is a woman of faith who believes Jesus can heal her daughter, which means that when she comes to meet Jesus, she is also a woman of hope.

Courage: despite the rebuff from the disciples and being seemingly ignored by Jesus, she becomes more confident and this gives her courage to persevere.

Perseverance: a good word that covers her willingness to banter and bargain with Jesus, a persistence (and pestering) in her request which highly energises her perseverance.

Voice

The story comes from Matthew's Gospel, generally a 'thinking' gospel, usually straightforward and direct in style. There is a precedent in Genesis for the behaviour of the woman in pleading her cause. This is the story of Abraham bartering with God about how many will be spared in the destruction of Sodom and Gomorrah (Genesis 19). God seems to be enjoying the ritual of middle-eastern bargaining and ultimately grants Abraham's request. As does Jesus with this woman.

Other voices

There are others in the Gospels who approach Jesus with requests for healing, although these requests are for themselves. Bartimaeus, the blind man (Mark 10:45-52), is also shunted aside by Jesus' disciples, but Bartimaeus perseveres and Jesus asks for him to come forward. His sight is restored. A more hesitant woman is the woman suffering from a haemorrhage for twelve years (Mark 5:25-34). She has confidence in Jesus but does not want to approach him directly. Her faith means that it will be enough to touch the hem of his cloak. Though frightened and trembling, she is given health and peace.

Jesus

The Syro-Phoenician woman had faith in Jesus. What did she see in him? Clearly, someone who had power to heal. But, in Matthew's dramatic style, Jesus' first response is to say nothing. It is something the same with Bartimaeus. His point with the blind man is that he will respond to the need of the person, especially if they express it. He asks Bartimaeus, 'What would you have me do for you?' He does not impose on anyone. He responds to their express wish of faith. So, to highlight the great faith, which he praises, he engages in repartee with the woman, and she is every match for Jesus. The woman with the flow of blood expresses her recognition of Jesus as a healer through her touch. It was enough. Jesus felt power ebb out of him. The touch of faith draws out healing.

Deepening the meaning

1. Faith is not confined to a 'chosen people', nor to the lost sheep of the house of Israel. Do we recognise belief, faith and a good way of life in people of other religions, in people who profess no religion?
2. Here is a woman courageous enough to confront a male religious leader, confident to argue with him for what she hoped and believed in. How is the behaviour of the woman a challenge to us to stand up for what we believe?
3. She has been humiliated by Jesus' disciples, shunned by them. She perseveres and confidently faces the verbal interaction with Jesus, making her case. How is this woman one of the best examples of faith and authenticity in the Gospels?
4. She 'knows her place' and kneels at Jesus' feet. Is bargaining with God and with Jesus a helpful model of the prayer of petition?
5. But, not only is her faith rewarded with her daughter recovering, but she is singled out by Jesus as having great faith. Looking at our faith, could Jesus single each of us out as a person of great faith?

3. Martha

For *Lectio Divina*

When Martha heard that Jesus had come she went to meet him. Mary remained sitting in the house. Martha said to Jesus, 'If you had been here, my brother would not have died. But I know that even now, whatever you ask of God, he will grant you. 'Your brother' said Jesus to her 'will rise again.' Martha said, 'I know that he will rise again at the resurrection on the last day. Jesus said:

> 'I am the resurrection.
> If anyone believes in me, even though he dies he will live,
> and whoever lives and believes in me
> will never die.
> Do you believe this?'

'Yes, Lord,' she said 'I believe that you are the Christ, the Son of God, the one who was to come into this world.'

John 11:20-27

Themes

Carer
Grief
Friendship
Belief
Joy

Explanation

Carer: from Jesus' visit to Martha and Mary, we know that Martha is, above all, a practical carer, but has been warned not to worry and fret.

Grief: the Gospel story highlights grief, and the testing of faith, since word was sent to Jesus that Lazarus was ill, but he did not come. Martha grieves her brother's death, so much so, with her sister Mary, that Jesus wept.

Friendship: Martha is a person at ease with Jesus, even in this time of distress, reminding him that had he come, Lazarus may not have died. She is also in the style of those who bargain with God. And she remains practical, warning about the possible odour from the tomb.

Belief: even in her sorrow, she can proclaim confidently that she believes in the resurrection of the dead.

Joy: it is to Martha that Jesus makes one of his statements that has become one of the most important and most quoted: that he is the resurrection and the life. It is to Martha who used to worry and fret that he is able to make this statement and bring her joy.

Voice

Because the story of the raising of Lazarus comes at the eve of Jesus' passion and death, it is important as a resurrection story that will be fulfilled in Jesus' resurrection. Decades after the events and in the writing of John's Gospel, Martha must have been a significant woman of faith to be chosen for the key revelation of Jesus as the resurrection and the life. Carer for Jesus in his ministry, friend whom he could comfortably visit, she now is portrayed as a listener in faith to a significant message.

Other Voices

The story of Martha and Mary in Luke 10:38-42 is a story about contemplating before going into action. It immediately follows the story of the Good Samaritan, about going into action. The Lukan voice indicates that Martha should be more like Mary, her sister, a listener to God's Word before setting herself up as self-sacrificing, worrying and fretting. In her faith journey (from Luke's Gospel to John's), it is clear that she has followed what Jesus has suggested. While she hurries to Jesus when he arrives after the death of Lazarus (and Mary sits), she is a listener to the Word. As a post-script to this profound story, John 12 notes that at the meal to celebrate Lazarus' new life, Martha, the same and different, is still caring for the guests at table.

Jesus

Jesus is comfortable with Martha. He responds to her loving care and is at home with her hospitality. This does not stop him from speaking plainly to her about her over-busyness, urging her to a more listening and discerning approach to life. Jesus is still comfortable with her when he comes after Lazarus dies, speaking with her as a close friend, weeping with her, comforting her and strengthening her faith in him and in resurrection.

Deepening the meaning

1. Faith is in the heart and mind, but it is also seen in self-giving and hospitable care to those in need. How do we respond to Jesus telling Martha not to worry and fret? Are we busy, worrying and fretting?
2. The busy person has to learn that being busy and caring is not the be-all and end-all of life. It makes us self-focused and worrying rather than offering selfless love. How much danger is there in our worrying and fretting that we are more absorbed with ourselves and our problems?
3. Faith means friendship with Jesus, being at ease with him, able to speak plainly, even chiding him, but always trusting. How had Martha changed when she went out to meet Jesus and speak about Lazarus?
4. Faith means being a realist, in learning to accept what has happened; grieving, but knowing that a life in faith means going on with life. How significant is it to us as it was to Martha that Jesus said he was the resurrection and the Life?
5. Being a faithful listener means openness, and being able to respond to God's Word which can bring both revelation and joy. How had Martha become more like the quiet and listening Mary?

4. Mary Magdalene

For *Lectio Divina*

Mary turned round and saw Jesus standing there, though she did not recognise him. Jesus said, 'Woman, why are you weeping? Who are you looking for?' Supposing him to be the gardener, she said, 'Sir, if you have taken him away, tell me where you have put him, and I will go and remove him.' Jesus said, 'Mary!' She knew him then and said to him in Hebrew, 'Rabbuni' - which means Master. Jesus said to her, 'Do not cling to me, because I have not yet ascended to the Father. But go and find the brothers, and tell them: 'I am ascending to my Father, to my God and your God'. So Mary of Magdala went and told the disciples that she had seen the Lord and that he had said these things to her.

John 20:11-18

Themes

Suffering
Search
Love
Apostle

Explanation

Suffering: at this stage of the passion story, Mary Magdalene has followed Jesus to Calvary and been present at the foot of the cross. She has mourned and helped with Jesus' burial. She has shared Jesus' suffering.

Search: still suffering, she has gone to the empty tomb. Finding it empty, she has still no realisation of resurrection, but deep down there is hope that something might be done and she continues to search.

Love: this has been her motivation since being healed of evil spirits and becoming a disciple, even to the cross when the others fled. At the sound of her name, Jesus' personal touch, she recognises him. She clings to him – a translation of Jesus' words could also be: you have to let me go.

Apostle: an apostle is one who witnessed Jesus' life, death and resurrection and has been sent out to proclaim this good news. Mary is the first resurrection apostle.

Voice

With the dominance of males in the time of Jesus, in public life and in religious roles, Mary Magdalene has a significant place in the Gospels. By the time of writing of John's Gospel, at the end of the first century, it is interesting (and challenging) to find that not only is Mary Magdalene singled out at the foot of the cross, but that her faith, her personal choice by Jesus, and his commissioning her to be the apostle of his resurrection are dramatised in this story.

Other Voices

There are various Bible traditions associated with the story of Mary Magdalene. The first may well be unfair, naming her as a prostitute, linking her with the sinful woman of Luke 7:36-50 who gatecrashes the dinner at the house of Simon the Pharisee and who anoints Jesus' feet and is forgiven her many sins. The older tradition is that of the prophet Hosea, who, in search of a wife, is led by God to a pagan shrine to marry Gomer, one of the shrine prostitutes. He loves her. She loves him but then turns away from him. In his dilemma, he discerns that he should not cast her off but forgive her and take her back. She became a symbol of the whole of Israel, sinful but beloved and forgiven. The other tradition is that of the Song of Songs 5:6-8 (used as a reading for the feast of Mary Magdalene, 22 July). She is the beloved of the fourth poem in the text who lost her beloved and goes searching for him, even suffering for him.

Jesus

In the Gospels, the resurrection story is the only time that Jesus speaks directly to Mary Magdalene (although the Luke passage already mentioned has a tradition of Jesus saying that her many sins are forgiven because she has loved so much even though the woman is not Mary Magdalene). There are two facets of Jesus' response to Mary's faith. The first is his friendship with her, one might say his affection for her, addressing her by name. The second is his confidence and trust in missioning her to be his resurrection apostle.

Deepening the Meaning

1. Mary's condition before she met Jesus, a woman afflicted who wanted healing. Do we pray prayers of healing for body and for spirit?
2. Mary as a disciple who (Luke 8) was prepared to give up her normal life to be a disciple and to care for Jesus and the apostles. How has becoming a follower of Jesus meant giving up parts of our lives?
3. Do we have Mary Magdalene moments in our pain and grieving as she did at the foot of the cross?
4. Mary and her grief for Jesus as she became part of the group of women who prepared Jesus' body for burial; her piety and devotion. Do we see that so much of our faith life is doing small things, devotion to others?
5. The searching Mary who was rewarded with a personal encounter with Jesus (his first resurrection encounter) and, in love and friendship, is an apostle of Jesus' good news. Have we experienced Mary Magdalene moments as we have shared our faith in Jesus who is Risen Lord?

5. Mary, Mother of Jesus

For *Lectio Divina*

The angel Gabriel was sent by God to a town in Galilee called Nazareth, to a virgin betrothed to a man named Joseph, of the House of David; and the virgin's name was Mary. He went in and said to her, 'Rejoice, so highly favoured! The Lord is with you.' She was deeply disturbed by these words and asked herself what this greeting could mean, but the angel said to her, 'Mary, do not be afraid; you have won God's favour. Listen! You are to conceive and bear a son and you must name him Jesus...'

'I am the handmaid of the Lord,' said Mary, 'let what you have said be done to me.'

Luke 1:26-32, 38

Themes

Graced
Openness
Concern
Commitment

Explanation

Graced: what theology calls the Immaculate Conception is a belief that Mary was beloved by God without hesitation from the first moment of her existence. As she grew, she was a grace-filled person. She had been filled with faith and love.

Openness: she responds instantly, listening to God's messenger (in contrast to Zechariah who had also been visited by Gabriel and who questioned what was happening and was made mute) wherever he might lead her.

Concern: but this openness did not mean that she had a blind, unquestioning faith. She does question, more of a concern as to how this message from God could happen given who she was and what her experience has been. The answer is the life of the Spirit.

Commitment: Mary's words have been used symbolically for many people to accept in faith what God asks.

Voice

The stories in Luke, chapters 1 and 2, are in the form of what me might call a meditative story about the birth of a great hero, using the storytelling forms used by contemporary writers in the Roman empire but drawing on many themes from the Old Testament. The annunciation narrative is a kind of scriptural poem, many strands that listeners and readers in the early church would recognise more readily than we do. Gabriel was the messenger from the Book of Daniel 9:21-27 for the fullness of time; there were annunciations to special mothers like those of Gideon and Samson; there are echoes of the prophet Zephaniah 3:14-18 and God's urging the Daughter of Jerusalem to rejoice... and many more. Mary is proposed as a singular woman of faith.

Other voices

In Matthew's Gospel, the focus is on Mary, the mother, and her child: the worries of her conceiving Jesus, the trip to Bethlehem, Jesus' birth, the visit of the Magi and their symbolic gifts, the flight to Egypt. In Luke's Gospel, Mary is someone who is filled with love and visits her cousin, Elizabeth, gives birth in Bethlehem and is visited by the outcast shepherds; she fulfils the rituals of the law, learns that Jesus has his mission – and ponders all this in her heart. In John's Gospel, she plays a symbolic role in being associated with Jesus' hour, anticipating it with her request at Cana, the abundant wine, present at the cross when the blood of Jesus, the wine of the Eucharist, is poured out. In the Acts of the Apostles, she is in the upper room, praying with the disciples, awaiting the Pentecost Spirit.

Jesus

While Matthew's and Luke's Gospels focus on Jesus before his birth and on his infancy, there are moments in the synoptic Gospels when Jesus sounds harsh when his mother and family try to see him, even when a woman in the crowd praises Mary for bearing him and suckling him. But, he makes the point that all his faith-disciples are his close family. They hear the Word of God and keep it. As we know, it is his mother who first and foremost heard the Word of God and kept it. The bond between mother and son is powerfully seen and felt in her request in Cana and his agreeing to her request. It is at the foot of the cross in entrusting Mary to John and John to Mary that Jesus affirms his mother as mother and as disciple and listener to the Word.

Deepening the meaning

1. Mary is an attentive listener, open to receive God's Word. How can this listening Mary be a model for our prayer?
2. Mary is on the margins, in danger of punishment because of her pregnancy, defended by Joseph. Have we given thought to this experience of Mary as outcast, even considered religiously criminal?
3. Mary is loving mother, pondering in her heart what she has experienced. She has heard the Word of God and kept it. How can this contemplating Mary be a model for our prayer?
4. Mary, called 'the mother of Jesus' at Cana, becomes part of the 'sacramental sign' of the changing of water into wine. What is the meaning of Mary's continuing prayer for us and intercession with her son?
5. Mary the mother and John, representing Jesus' disciples, are entrusted to each other as Jesus dies. What is the meaning of Mary, Mother of the Church?

2. STORIES OF FAITH

1. *Abraham*

For *Lectio Divina*

The Lord said to Abram, 'Leave your country, your family and your father's house, for the land I will show you. I will make you a great nation. I will bless you and make your name so famous that it will be used as a blessing.

> I will bless those who bless you:
> I will curse those who slight you.
> All the tribes of the earth
> shall bless themselves by you.'

So Abram went as the Lord told him.

Genesis 12:1-3

Themes

Abram the patriarch
Call
Blessing
Journey

Explanation

Abram the patriarch: Before he was given the name Abraham by the Lord, Abram dwelt with his clan on the Persian Gulf. He was old, had a wife Sarai, his nephew Lot, and their possessions. He worshipped a local god.

Call: Abram's religious experience of his God was personalised, an interior spiritual experience. This experience was a call, told in story as a call from the Lord, Abram hearing an inner voice that was so powerful there was nothing he could do but respond.

Blessing: the call also included a sense of destiny for Abram and his descendants, a protective providence for Abram from the Lord. There was material blessing, a new land, a growing people, admiration from other peoples and blessings for those who blessed Abram – and rejection for those who cursed him. But, the blessing was also spiritual. The description of the relationship between Abram and the Lord was one of spiritual alertness, attentiveness and obedience in action.

Journey: the journey has centuries of history as an image of life. Any divine call leads to a personal, sometimes a communal journey into new territory, the reality and symbol of a new life.

Voice

The books of the Pentateuch were written comparatively late in Israel's history, drawing on oral traditions, attempting – often through tales and sagas - to interpret Israel's choice by God and the people's sacred history. This passage is the opening of the sagas about Abraham.

Other voices

This call passage is developed when Abram has a vision (Genesis 15:1-21) and the Lord pledges fidelity to Abram, seals a covenant with him, dramatised by the halving of the covenant victim, warding off birds of prey and the symbolic passing through of the Lord in the symbol of fire. The first promises are now repeated and developed.

By the time that the Lord visits Sodom and is to punish the people, we see that Abraham (now named) has such an intimacy with the Lord that he can go through a Semitic bargaining process with great confidence, whittling down the number of just men that the Lord will spare. Faith grows in intimacy with God.

In his letters, Paul refers to Abraham as 'father in faith' because of his faith-response to the Lord which justified him in God's eyes (Romans 4:1-3)

Jesus

Jesus often refers to Abraham and his faith, referring, for instance, to this in refuting the arguments against life after death (Mark 12:26). In the parable of Dives and Lazarus, the afterlife is described as being with Abraham (Luke 16:19-31). And in John's Gospel, the religious leaders taunt him, asking him if he is greater than our father Abraham. Jesus replies with asserting himself, 'Before Abraham ever was, I am' (John 8:52-58). He is one with the Father, the God who reveals, 'I am', the living God.

Deepening the meaning

1. God takes the initiative in Abram's call, an initiative we might name as a call of grace, inviting Abram to respond in faith, which he does. Are we comfortable in using the word 'grace' in talking about our lives?
2. God's initiative can be described as blessing. The blessing is not merited, but God calls nonetheless. What have we experienced as blessings in our lives?
3. The response of faith for Abram was experienced interiorly as a personal call, an invitation so strong that he could not respond otherwise but to do what God asked. Can we recall our significant personal calls to faith and action?
4. The response of faith also leads to action, moving away from the past, a new destination, a willing moving into the unknown. Can we trace such steps in our journey of faith?
5. The response of faith also leads to a journey. This may not be a physical journey (although for most of us, it is). It may be a personal and profound spiritual journey even if we remain in the one place. And it may be a journey that takes others, family, community, with us. How have we experienced journeys literal, spiritual, in our lives?

2. Isaiah

For *Lectio Divina*

I saw the Lord seated on a high throne; his train filled the sanctuary; above him stood Seraphs, each one with six wings: two to cover its face, two to cover its feet and two for flying.
And they cried out to one to another in this way,

> 'Holy, holy, holy is the Lord of hosts.
> His glory fills the whole earth.'

The foundations of the threshold shook with the voice of the one who cried out, and the temple was filled with smoke. I said:

> 'What are wretched state I am in! I am lost,
> For I am a man of unclean lips
> And I live among a people of unclean lips,
> and my eyes have looked at the King, the Lord of hosts.'

Then one of the Seraphs flew to me, holding in his hand a live coal which he had taken from the altar with a pair of tongs. With this he touched my mouth and said:

> 'See now, this has touched your lips,
> your sin is taken away,
> your iniquity is purged.'

Then I heard the voice of the Lord saying:

> 'Whom shall I send? Who will be our messenger?'

I answered, 'Here I am, send me.'

Isaiah 6:1-9

Themes

Temple
Prophet
Ritual
Cleansing
Commitment

Explanation

Temple: the most sacred place of faith and worship, the place where God dwells.

Prophet: Isaiah had been personally called by God. The invitation is renewed and the prophet consents.

Ritual: the text describes different aspects of this solemn profession of faith and commitment in the sacred place.

Cleansing: with the tradition of incense, ministers at the altar and a purification, symbolically, of the prophet's lips, a confession.

Commitment: the religious experience in the temple is solemn and profound, so that the prophet's faith breaks forth in an offering to speak on behalf of God.

Voice

Isaiah was one of the earliest classical prophets, whose oracles were recorded and edited, along with oracles by anonymous disciples, into the book we now have. The classic prophets usually have a 'call' section to show how the prophet's religious experience of God coloured his message and its communication.

Other voices

Jeremiah (chapter 1:4-10) was a major classical prophet. His call happened when he was young. He felt unwilling to respond, not able to be a prophet, even though he had been consecrated from his birth. God puts his words into Jeremiah's mouth and sends him to communicate God's message.

Ezekiel was also a major classical prophet. However, his call story seems quite exotic, full of symbolic imagery that he could draw on for his message (Ezekiel 1:4-28).

Jesus

Jesus had his own Temple experience at the age of twelve, a consequence of his Bar Mitzvah, becoming an adult in the community, a proclaimer of the Word (Luke 2:41-50).

Jesus was also linked in Matthew's Gospel (1:22-23) with the book of Isaiah 7:14, where a symbol was offered to Israel for the fullness of time, a maiden who was pregnant and gave birth to a son who was Emmanuel, 'God is with us'.

The Servant of the book of Isaiah was a model for the New Testament writers, someone beloved and chosen, who would heal, speak God's Word but would be opposed, insulted and tortured, finally dying for others.

Deepening the meaning

1. The call of Isaiah is one of the most solemn in the scriptures, highlighting the sacredness of a call and its faith-response. Do we know the hymn 'Hear I am, Lord', use it as a prayer?
2. The call to faith and commitment requires a purification, symbolically, on the lips for a mission of purity and authenticity. Can we recall moments of 'purification', what they were, their impact? The consequences?
3. Faith deepens the awareness of God: Isaiah sees God as great, a God of grandeur in the halls of the temple and its ritual incense, a God who is holy/sacred. What has been the sense of the sacred in our lives?
4. Isaiah was a statesman in Israel, an important figure but he discovers that this means little in God's presence. No matter how important we are – or think we are – have we had Isaiah moments when conscious of our limitations in God's eyes?
5. The profound experience of the call and faith of Isaiah was not just personal, interior. His new consciousness of God alerted him to a further call, of being asked to commit himself in action. His faith response is 'Send me'. When have we had the experience of saying to God, 'Send me'?

3. The woman at the well

For *Lectio Divina*

The woman said to him, 'I know that Messiah - that is, Christ – is coming; and when he comes he will tell us everything'. 'I who am speaking to you', said Jesus, 'I am he.'

John 4:25-26

Themes

Samaritan
The well at Sychar
Living water
Recognition
Faith

Explanation

Samaritan woman: her encounter with Jesus is one of the longest stories in the Gospels. The Samaritans and the Jews were enemies for many centuries. Yet Jesus chose to travel from Galilee to Jerusalem through Samaria – and favoured Samaritans in the parable of The Good Samaritan and that one of the ten lepers who were cured was a Samaritan (Luke 17:11-19).

The well at Sychar: a symbol of the old tradition of Jews and Samaritans having lineage from the patriarchs (Genesis 33:18-20) where Jacob buys land at Shechem and erects an altar, the well there later known as Joseph's well. The woman will defend the traditions, especially that of worshipping on Mt Gerazim instead of Jerusalem.

Living water: water was a key symbol of the Old Testament, Creation 'over the waters', Exodus and the Red Sea, washing and purification. Water was a sacred symbol. Jesus identifies with it as a means of refreshment and life. Water is a key symbol of the New Testament: the Jordan, baptism, cup of cold water, water into wine, water and the Spirit.

Recognition: this story of the woman at the well is one of a faith journey. It is not something she chose. Rather, she is invited to faith.

'Give me a drink.' The disciples are going to be scandalised by Jesus talking to the woman and drinking. She is an unlikely disciples. Jesus questions her. She responds, realised that he is special, a prophet, who tells her about her marriages. He reveals that he is the living water. This water is something she wants.

Faith: Faith is an invitation, offered in the context of our lives, our ordinary lives. But, there is the promise of something special. This is what the woman wants. And, while she shares her faith with the townspeople, they do not have much regard for her and declare that they have responded in faith after hearing Jesus.

Voice

With John's Gospel being finally written many decades after the death of Jesus, some stories became more and more important in John's community. This one is a Samaritan story, a woman's story, the obtuseness of Jesus' disciples in not recognising what had happened.

Other Voices

Water is a theme in John's Gospel: at Cana, at the well, at the pool of Bethesda, at the pool of Siloam, the washing of the feet, water from the side of Christ. John's Gospel uses the language of 'signs and wonders'. Water is associated with many of these signs.

Jesus

There is quite a deal of dialogue in John's Gospels and we hear Jesus speak: at Cana, with Nicodemus, with the man born blind, with Martha after the death of Lazarus, with the Magdalene in the garden, with Thomas. While the narratives are stylised, a picture of Jesus emerges from these encounters, very personal, often affectionate, challenging and soothing, and offering the gift of faith.

Deepening the meaning

1. The invitation to faith can be quite unexpected, offered to someone considered the least likely. Apart from ourselves, have we seen conversion experiences in seemingly unlikely people?
2. The story dramatizes the personal approach of Jesus and the gift of faith. What is the appeal of this story of the woman at the well?

3. The story dramatises the different stages of response of the woman, accosted by a stranger, his unusual request of a Samaritan and a woman, her response to his talk of water, the personal challenge and her defensiveness, listening to the words of Jesus about living water... When have we experienced 'prods' to conversion in our lives?
4. Jesus as living water. How is this a symbolic image, in view of the Old Testament tradition of water, cleansing, oasis in the desert, satisfying thirst?
5. The faith enthusiasm of the villagers – and their disregard for the woman who nevertheless was the one who had encountered Jesus. How best to nurture those who are at the beginning of their faith journey?

4. Peter

For *Lectio Divina*

When Jesus came to the region of Caesarea Philippi, he put this question to his disciples, 'Who do people say the Son of Man is?' And they said, 'Some say he is John the Baptist, some Elijah, and others Jeremiah or one of the prophets'. 'But you', he said, 'who do you say I am?' Then Simon Peter spoke up, 'You are the Christ', he said, 'the Son of the living God.' Jesus replied, 'Simon, son of Jonah, you are happy man! Because it was not flesh and blood that revealed this to you but my Father in heaven.'

Matthew 16:13-17

Themes

The apostles
Jesus and the prophets
Test of faith
Peter and the twelve
Revelation and faith

Explanation

The Apostles: the apostles are models of faith, each in his different way (including a failure, Judas). They were called by name, sometimes a brief description given, but they shared in Jesus' ministry, saw him for a long period of time in close-up. Ultimately, they were to be the new covenant leaders of the new tribes of Israel.

Jesus and the prophets: many of the things that Jesus did reminded people of the prophets, for instance his raising of the son of the widow of Naim reminded them of Elijah raising a widow's son. His reputation spread and people were asking whether he was one of the prophets returned to earth.

Test of faith: initial experiences of faith can be very simple, very enthusiastic. Call and discipleship can produce an initial 'high'. But, faith must be deepened, questioned, examined. This episode was an occasion for testing faith and what it meant and how they recognised Jesus.

Peter and the twelve: already Peter had been singled out by Jesus as a leader of the twelve, a spokesperson for them. In Matthew's Gospel, this is a key moment, not only because of Peter's profession but for the words that Jesus offers him as a consequence. He is the rock on which the church is built. He is given the keys of the kingdom.

Revelation and faith: we are reminded that faith is not self-generated. It is a gift. We can examine, reflect, see the credibility of faith. But faith is not something just of 'flesh and blood'. It is a gift where God chooses, calls and graces.

Voice

The Gospel of Matthew came from the early Jewish community whose faith was being tested. The Gospel goes back to Old Testament quotations and references to situate Jesus and faith in him in the Old Testament context. As was often said in relation to Jesus and Old Testament figures, 'A greater than… is here'. Jesus is greater than all the prophets. He is the fulfilment of the prophets and God's presence on earth.

Other voices

Peter is a fisherman, with little education and, as he said, a sinful man. Yet, it is he who is called to follow Jesus, and to be a model of what discipleship is, even with so many faults and lapses.

Peter is called to share in special experiences with Jesus, especially the vision of the transfiguration where Jesus is seen as the fulfilment of prophecy (symbolised by Elijah) and of the law (symbolised by Moses).

The impetuous Peter refuses to have his feet washed, then wants complete washing, professes loyalty, then denies Jesus, and is asked finally whether he loves Jesus – and receives his mission of leadership, tending the flock.

Jesus

While Jesus has chosen Peter as a leader of the Twelve, we see his choices - at the Sea of Galilee - of Andrew, James and John. James and John are privileged witnesses of the Transfiguration, the raising of the daughter of Jairus, the agony in the garden. John is beloved and stands at the foot of the cross. Others have speaking roles: Andrew and Philip for the feeding of the 5000, Philip, Thomas and Jude and their asking questions at the Last Supper.

Deepening the meaning

1. There are key moments in life when our private faith has to declare itself publicly, to express what we truly believe and understand. Considering our public lives as Christians, do we declare ourselves, our faith, belief, spirituality?
2. We are Peter-like in our lives and in our faith, whether we are in leadership roles or not. Despite many failings, how do we respond when are we asked to transcend our limitations and make faith statements in word and action?
3. We have our moments with the key Jesus-question, 'Who do you say I am?'. What is our answer?
4. Our answer is grounded in our experience of Jesus, what is our experience? How grounded in God's Word?
5. Once we have answered the Jesus question - whether in a peak experience or day-by-day - what responsibilities are given to us as disciples?

5. Witnesses to the Resurrection: Mary Magdalene and Thomas

For *Lectio Divina*

Jesus said, 'Mary... Go and find the brothers, and tell them: I am ascending to my Father and to your Father, to my God and your God.' So Mary of Magdala went and told the disciples that she had seen the Lord and that he had said these things to her...

'Peace be with you.' Then Jesus spoke to Thomas, 'Put your finger here; look, here are my hands. Give me your hand; put it into my side. Doubt no longer but believe.' Thomas replied, 'my Lord and my God!'

John 20:17-18, 27-28

Themes

The risen Lord
Mary Magdalene
Witness to the resurrection
Thomas
Seeing and believing

Explanation

The Risen Lord: after a public ministry of three years, Jesus dies on the cross, breathing forth his spirit but, having surrendered himself to the Father, he now has a new life which transcends the old. And it is the Risen Lord who commands faith.

Mary Magdalene: there is much confusion about Mary of Magdala. She is often confused with Mary sister of Martha and the woman, the sinner of Luke 12 (and sometimes, the woman taken in adultery in John 8). Mary of Magdala had experienced some evil spirits or spirits of disturbance in her which Jesus cast out. She was at the foot of the cross on Calvary and now searches for Jesus.

Witness to the Resurrection: this was the main criterion for the authenticity of the chosen twelve apostles and for the replacement for Judas. The striking aspect of John 20 is that the woman, Mary, is the chosen witness to the resurrection. It is she who lets Peter and John know what has happened.

Thomas: a forthright personality, one of the twelve, but here finding his most memorable moment, representing the doubts of the apostles and disciples.

Seeing and believing: Jesus makes the important point that those who see the Risen Lord are blessed, but happy are those who have not seen and yet believe.

Voice

These are two key Resurrection stories, John's key stories. The narratives come at the end of the first Christian century, stories chosen in retrospect that would support faith journeys at this time of the development of the church. In view of what was reported in John's Gospel, Mary being at the foot of the cross and then so involved in the search for Jesus, this is quite surprising. It would seem that her memory had grown stronger over the decades.

Thomas had made several appearances, and is even among the group fishing in Galilee (and named immediately after Peter) after the Resurrection. He becomes the symbol of doubt and then of immediate faith.

Other voices

Apart from the references in John's passion and resurrection stories, the other mention of Mary Magdalene is among the group of women who followed Jesus and ministered to him and the disciples (Luke 8:1-3).

Thomas was eager to go to suffer with Jesus when he delays going to visit Lazarus, asking the question at the Last Discourse, which receives the answer, 'I am the way, the truth and the life'. And now the doubting Thomas who wants to see and touch in order to believe.

Jesus

In chapter 20 of John, after Mary's initial search and Peter and John running to the tomb, there are three main stories. Jesus is revealed as risen, walking in the garden and encountering Mary, naming her. He says she must not cling to him, or, 'you should let me go', as he has to go to the Father.

Then there is the story of Jesus appearing to the eleven, breathing on them and giving his peace and his gift of forgiveness.

The Thomas story follows and the finale to the original end of the Gospel. 'These signs are recorded so that you may believe that Jesus is the Christ, the Son of God, and the believing this you may have life through his name.'

Deepening the meaning

1. Jesus of Nazareth has become the Risen Lord. We believe in Jesus of Nazareth. What does it mean to believe in the Risen Lord?
2. What is the significance of Mary of Magdala being the first witness to the resurrection? And Jesus' tender speaking with her and commissioning her as witness?
3. How is Thomas a model of our own doubts, frustrations and the mystery of our faith?
4. The nature of Thomas' faith experience, a reversal of his attitude moments before, a profound change, the joy that he discovers he is able to believe.
5. What is the quality of faith of those who do not see but believe?

THROUGHOUT THE YEAR

1. JUSTICE

1. Justice and the Prophet Amos

For *Lectio Divina*

The Lord says this:

> For the three crimes, the four crimes, of Israel
> I have made my decree and will not relent:
> because they have sold the virtuous man for silver
> and the poor man for a pair of sandals,
> because they trample on the heads of ordinary people
> and push the poor out of their path.
>
> *Amos 2:6-7*

Themes

Amos
Crimes
My decree
The poor
Ordinary people

Explanation

Amos: a prophet around the year 740 BC, someone who worked the land, was down-to-earth, spoke out about injustices.

Crimes: in the first two chapters of the book of Amos, the prophet has a series of oracles against the sinfulness of the territories around Israel, their three crimes and four crimes, and then centres on Judaea and then on the northern kingdom of Israel where he lived.

My decree: this is the decree of the God of Justice, true to his people, but true to himself, acknowledging the infidelity to the covenant by the people and their injustice.

The poor: throughout his oracles, the prophet singles out those who are poor, needy, and contrasts them with the wealthy and the self-indulgent.

Ordinary people: a key phrase for the message of Justice and the oppression of the arrogant and the wealthy against the poor, the ordinary people.

Voice

Amos was the first of the so-called classical prophets, the prophets whose oracles were written down. His mission was to warn the inhabitants of the Northern Kingdom that the consequences of their covenant infidelity and their oppression of the poor had led them to a worldliness that would be their downfall and cause the invasion of an enemy and the dispersion of the people – which happened.

Other voices

All the prophets spoke about issues of Justice and the people's selfish infidelity, from lengthy passages in the prophet Isaiah, to the lamentations of Jeremiah (why do sinners always prosper?). Even Hosea, the prophet of God's tender love, has some severe passages about injustice, including God saying 'what I want is obedience not sacrifice'.

Jesus

Perhaps the most telling image of justice is that of the widow who puts her small coin in the collection box, all that she has, for the poor. In the Beatitudes, Jesus praises those who hunger and thirst for Justice.

Deepening the meaning

1. In most translations of Amos, the language is quite straightforward; some of the condemnation passages in the Jerusalem Bible translation take on a more poetic and rhetorical tone which enhances the tone of Amos but, perhaps, diminishes his demands. What is the impact of the blunt Amos, his view on sinfulness and injustice?
2. While Amos is the Prophet of Justice, and justifies his role of criticism against the condemnations by the authorities (3:3-8), he mixes some mercy with God's demands of justice and sometimes offers hymns of praise to God and creation. Can we find the passages of mercy that temper the justice?

3. Amos, in the prophetic action tradition, nevertheless introduces this Justice theme into the writings of the prophets. The prophets will take it for granted that Justice and sins against Justice are a key covenant concern. Do we? In the injustices in today's world?

4. Amos highlights the sinfulness of treading on the heads of ordinary people by talking about the atrocities committed by other countries. Israel's oppression of the poor, therefore, is an atrocity. The Jerusalem Bible has one of the most arresting translations of one of Amos's threats: "See then how I am going to crush you into the ground as the threshing-sledge crashes when clogged by straw" (Amos 2:13). What is our experience of being poor – and how just and generous is our response to poverty today?

5. Amos also introduces the idea of the Day of the Lord, the day of reckoning when people will have to face their sinfulness, take the opportunity to repent – and the name of those who are faithful and repent is "the remnant". How dramatic is the impact of Amos' severe words and challenges about justice?

2. Justice and the Sermon on the Mount

For *Lectio Divina*

Why do you observe the splinter in your brother's eye and never noticed the plank in your own? How dare you say to your brother, "Let me take the splinter out of your eye", when all the time there is a plank in your own? Hypocrite! Take the plank out of your own eye first, and then you will see clearly enough to take the splinter out of your brother's eye.

Matthew 7:4-5

Themes

Judgment
Arrogance
Splinters and planks
Self-examination
Peace and reconciliation

Explanation

Judgment: the passage quoted follows Jesus' injunction that we should not judge so that we will not be judged. With judgments on others comes the possibility for injustice.

Arrogance: looking at the faults and failings of others and judging them without doing the same towards oneself is an arrogance that leads to injustice.

Splinters and planks: this is one of Jesus most famous metaphors, well-remembered, especially for the image of the plank in the eye of the person who judges and is unjust.

Self-examination: if there is to be harmony, peace and reconciliation, then self-examination, finding one's own planks, can be a basis for Justice.

Peace and reconciliation: so much hostility comes from arrogance and judgments on others. Jesus' advice about splinters and planks is the beginning of a process that can lead to peace and reconciliation.

Voice

Much of Matthew's Gospel consists of sermons, the most famous of which is the Sermon on the Mount. it is a collection of Jesus' sayings, direct injunctions, small parables and metaphors to back up the injunctions, and Jesus saying that he has not come to take away anything from the old law but to bring it to perfection, the grounding for Christian morality.

Other voices

So much of the old law is found in the Pentateuch, in Exodus, Leviticus, Deuteronomy. There are the absolute commands of the Decalogue. There is all kind of case law in Exodus and Leviticus. A variation on the Sermon on the Mount can be found in Luke 6, a sermon on the plain, reiterating the themes of Matthew 5 to 8.

Jesus

In the infancy narratives of Matthew's Gospel, there are parallels between Jesus and Moses. Moses also appears in the transfiguration narrative, the symbol of the Old Testament law. Commentators see Jesus in going up the mountain for this Sermon on the Mount as parallel to Moses at Mt Sinai, going up to the Lord and receiving the Law.

Deepening the meaning

1. The Sermon on the Mount has been most significant in the Christian tradition. But, it has also been admired over the centuries by those who did not have Christian faith. It is seen as a compendium of the finest moral injunctions. For Christians, how is it an inspiration for Christ-like behaviour?

2. This passage comes in the context of judging – and Jesus said we should not judge. So much hostility, an eye for an eye, comes from the harshest judgments which lead to attack and warfare, so much of it unjust. Does an eye for an eye influence our response to those who offend us? Why?

3. The passage also comes in the Sermon on the Mount context of a rejection of any law of retaliation. When an aggressor removes the plank from their own eye, they can see more clearly and deal with

the splinter in the eye of the enemy. What are the planks in our eyes? How do they influence us to make harsh judgments?

4. In this passage, Jesus actually refers to splinters in the eye of a brother or sister, highlighting that all men and women should be in harmony rather than hostility and injustice. Where has there been leadership in the Church in recent times for harmony?

5. One of the key elements in the pursuit of justice is peace and reconciliation. How strong a motivation in our life is peace and reconciliation?

3. Labourers in the vineyard

For *Lectio Divina*

"Call the workers and pay them their wages, starting with the last arrivals and ending with the first. So those who were hired at about the eleventh hour came forward and received one denarius each. When the first came, they expected to get more, but they too received one denarius each. They took it, but grumbled at the landowner. "The men who came last" they said "have done only one hour, and you have treated them the same as us, though we have done a heavy day's work in all the heat." He answered one of them and said, "My friend, I am not being unjust to you; did we not agree on one denarius? Take your earnings and go. I choose to pay the last as much as I pay you. Have I no right to do what I like with my own? Why be envious because I am generous?"

Matthew 20:8-16

Themes

Landowner
Workers
Just wages
Equality in wages
Fairness and generosity

Explanation

Landowner: landowners like this and owners of property are a feature of Jesus' parables.

Workers: the workers from the drama contrast with the landowner, the kind of dramatic contrast that Jesus uses in his parables.

Just wages: the landowner is presented as a fair man, offering what is considered a fair and just wage, the workers accepting it. The foundation is laid for the final message of the parable.

Equality in wages: Jesus tells the parable in such a way that audiences listening might expect a bonus for those who had worked during the heat of the day. Jesus' parables usually subvert the listeners' expectations and lead them further.

Fairness and generosity: the landowner's decision to give the late comers the same wage does not break any contract, does not break any agreement for fairness. The landowner is entitled to be generous – Justice is not the only principle involved.

Voice

The parable is found only in Matthew's Gospel, an emphasis on working conditions, justice and fairness with the bonus of generosity. Matthew's Gospel tends to present its stories straightforwardly, an emphasis on clarity, with reasonable principles.

Other voices

This parable can be related to the parable of the talents in both Matthew and Luke, a focus on money, investment, work, just reward and generosity.

Jesus

Each of the Gospels has what may what one might call a different voice for Jesus, a more humane and emotional voice in Luke, matter of fact in detail in Mark, sometimes mystical and discursive in John. The voice of Jesus, as in this parable, in Matthew's Gospel is very clear, logical, no-frills.

Deepening the meaning

1. This is a parable unique to Matthew's Gospel, harking back to laws in books like Leviticus and Deuteronomy about owners, workers and just payment. It is Jesus' parable on distributive justice and fair work and fair wage. What has been the Church's teaching on work and justice? Do we know it and act on it?

2. Jesus makes the story more dramatic by having the landowner go out at various times during the day and hiring people. The workplace is a vineyard, an image popular in the Old Testament (Isaiah 5) and throughout the Gospels. How do we react to the landowner's way of dealing with wages? Justice? Generosity?

3. One aspect of Justice is distributive justice, with an emphasis on fairness, and an emphasis on equality and inequality in the distribution of benefits. How fair are we in dealing with others?

4. But distributive justice is only one aspect of Justice and can be transcended, as here, by generosity. Are we generous? Is today's society generous – toward which groups, and for which groups is there little generosity?

5. How is Jesus indicating by the parable that generosity and abundance is also a sound principle? A generosity of spirit, drawing on abundance for the benefit of others?

4. Justice and judgment

For *Lectio Divina*

Come, you whom my Father has blessed, take for your heritage the kingdom prepared for you since the foundation of the world. For I was hungry and you gave me food; I was thirsty and you gave me drink; I was a stranger and you made me welcome; naked, and you clothed me, sick and you visited me, in prison and you came to see me. Than the virtuous will say to him in reply, "Lord, when did we see you hungry and feed you; or thirsty and give you drink? When did we see you a stranger and make you welcome; naked and clothe you; sick or in prison and go to see you?" And the King will answer, "I tell you solemnly, insofar as you did this to one of the least of these brothers of mine, you did it to me".

Matthew 25:34-40

Themes

The just judge
Heritage of the just
Actions of the just
Justice for ordinary people
Justice and love for others

Explanation

The just judge: Jesus is pictured as the King, his subjects coming before him and his taking stock of their lives; he is the Shepherd separating sheep from goats.

Heritage of the just: to be called into the kingdom (the reign) and find their place there. The Kingdom of God, the Kingdom of heaven, is a kingdom of Justice.

Actions of the just: the poor in spirit of the Beatitudes, of those for whom justice is done by the just.

Justice for ordinary people: a catalogue of good actions - food and drink, welcome to strangers, clothing the naked, visiting the sick and prisoners - is honouring ordinary people in their needs.

Justice and love for others: this is the gospel invitation to see the face and features of Jesus in those who are poor and oppressed.

Voice

This is the voice of Matthew's Gospel, the Eschatological Discourse, a focus on the final times, apocalyptic times, times of judgment as well as a reckoning, as in the preceding parables of the ten bridesmaids and the parable of the talents.

Other voices

This parable of the last judgment finds its origins in Ezekiel 34 - his chapter on sheep where the shepherd separates the sheep from the goats. In view of recent church experiences of sexual abuse against children, the texts about the abuse of children and a millstone around the neck of the abusers can be connected to this parable.

Jesus

This is a stern voice of Jesus from Matthew's Gospel, taking up many sayings from the Sermon on the Mount, and following through with such parables as that of the unjust steward. Some of these Justice messages can be found in Luke 16, with the parable of the poor man and the rich man as well as the manipulative steward who, to protect himself, urges clients to change the amounts on their accounts.

Deepening the meaning

1. This is the last passage in Matthew's Gospel before the passion narratives. To that extent it is a dramatic climax to the Gospel. How cut and dried does this parable seem? Any place for compassion?

2. There is an Eschatological tone in the introduction to the parable, with the Son of Man coming in glory, escorted by the angels (echoes of Daniel 7) and holding a judgment that is not of this earth. How does this parable turn our attention to justice in this life and the consequences for our eternal life?

3. While this might seem unjust to the goats - are they being scapegoats again? - they are being used for the metaphor for those who are good and those who are evil, those who are on the right, those who are on the left. The origins of this are in Ezekiel 34. How do we respond to those who want to take the parable absolutely?

4. When preparing a list of justice issues, how is Jesus' catalogue in

this chapter of Matthew a good beginning, for justice and charity at home and to neighbours?

5. The actions of the sheep, praised by Jesus, are for entry into the Kingdom of Heaven – but how do they also make the reign of God present on earth?

5. What is good has been explained to you

For *Lectio Divina*
What is good has been explained to you; this is what Yahweh asks of you:
only this: to act justly,
to love tenderly
and to walk humbly with your God.

Micah 6:8

Themes
Micah
Covenant good
Acting justly
Loving tenderly
Walking humbly with God

Explanation
Micah: a prophet who comes at the end of the first Covenant crisis, the infidelity of Israel, the attack of the Assyrians, the dispersing of Israel, 700 BC, a prophet in the tradition of Amos and Hosea, conscious of Justice, but offering this well-known and favoured summing up of the spirituality of the time.

Covenant good: Micah is not just offering a sensible way of life, even a sensible spirituality of life. he is speaking about Covenant good, Covenant spirituality, a summation of the prophets Isaiah, Amos, Hosea.

Acting justly: the summary of the message of Amos.

Loving tenderly: the summary of the message of Hosea.

Walking humbly with God: the spirit of the prophet Isaiah, the statesman, who humbled himself asking to be sent as God's messenger.

Voice
The voice of Micah is the voice of the experience of an invasion, of Israel's fickleness, the call to repentance by the prophets, the doom for the people – and of hope for the future.

Other voices

These themes will be developed by later prophets, especially the more personalised oracles of Jeremiah, Ezekiel, and minor prophets, especially Zephaniah.

Jesus

Jesus proclaims Justice in the Kingdom/ Reign of God, justice issues being the criteria for entry into the Kingdom. Jesus, especially in the Gospel of Luke, shows the loving tenderness of the prophet Hosea in the story of the woman who was a sinner (Luke 7:36-50), the parable of the prodigal son (Luke 15) and the story of Zacchaeus (Luke 19). It is the theme of the story of the woman taken in adultery (John 8).

Deepening the meaning

1. While this is a passage well-loved by many, it might be seen as a desperate prayer after disastrous experiences. How can it be seen as a prayer of hope and aspiration?
2. How can this passage be seen as offering an agenda, wide-ranging from Justice to Love – but not in any self-promoting sense, but discerning and walking humbly with God?
3. The basis for acting justly is a response to God's justice and fairness and abundance, not merely a going around doing good that satisfies the person doing good. How well do we understand this spirituality of justice?
4. Loving tenderly can sound very emotional, and it is, but this love is also compassion. How is this tender love of God a reaching out in covenant fidelity, an offering of help and healing in love?
5. Walking humbly is not merely a spirituality of subservience. It is a spirituality that is well-grounded (from the meaning of the origin in *humus*, the ground), and authentic companionship with God. How well do we understand this true meaning of humility and authenticity?

2. JESUS' LEADERSHIP

1. Jesus emptied himself of his divinity

For *Lectio Divina*

His state was divine,
yet he did not cling
to his equality with God
but emptied himself
to assume the condition of a slave,
and became as we are;
and being as all are,
he was humbler yet,
even into accepting death,
death on a cross.
But God raised him high
and gave him the name
which is above all other names
so that all beings
in the heavens, on earth and in the underworld,
should bend the knee of the name of Jesus
and that every tongue should acclaim
Jesus Christ as Lord,
to the glory of God the Father.

Philippians 2:6-11

Themes

His divine state
Equality with God
Emptied himself
Being as we are
Death on the cross

Explanation

His divine state: in this hymn about the incarnation, the starting premise is Jesus and his divinity.

Equality with God: and the nature of this divinity is that he is one with the Father.

Emptied himself: an early understanding of the incarnation, that not only did Jesus come to earth as human, but he let go of his divinity, emptying himself.

Being as we are: Jesus is fully human, sharing our nature and our human experiences.

Death on the cross: Jesus, divine, who could be referred to as master, in his incarnate leadership is willing to share the utmost human experiences of suffering.

Voice

The letter to the Philippians is one of the later letters of St Paul, acknowledging his imprisonment, acknowledging his age, becoming ready for his death. These words seem to come from an early Christian hymn honouring Jesus and the incarnation.

Other voices

There are other early hymns amongst the New Testament letters: a creation hymn focusing on Jesus as the image of God (Colossians 1:15-20); two in 1 Timothy 3:16 and 6:15-16.

Jesus

There are many references to Jesus being one with the Father but also, in his incarnation, sharing human suffering. The passion narratives are the foremost examples but to experience the suffering humanity of Jesus in the face of death, the various agony in the garden passages are key. As are the descriptions of his suffering before going to Calvary, his carrying the cross to Calvary, his feelings of desolation and abandonment on the cross but the final consent to his mission as Jesus breathes forth his spirit.

Deepening the meaning

1. This hymn must have been significant in the early Christian communities for it to be quoted in this letter by Paul. it is a celebration of Jesus: it emphasises his divinity, his equality with

God but it moves on to the incarnation, the profound experience of Jesus as a human being, which led to his death on the cross. But the end of incarnation is in resurrection and glorification. How valuable is this hymn as a frequent prayer?
2. There is a Greek word for this emptying, *kenosis*, which indicates the profound will of Jesus in moving away from his unique oneness with the Father in the Spirit and embracing human nature. What does reflecting on 'kenosis' reveal about Jesus and his life and death?
3. In terms of Jesus' leadership, it is based on this emptying of himself and his status as God. How does his becoming human show that leadership is an emptying of self, a true humility and grounding on the earth, an authentic acknowledgement of himself and his role in leading the Twelve and his disciples?
4. The implication of leadership like that of Jesus is suffering and even martyrdom.
5. While there is suffering in leadership on earth, God raises Jesus and, therefore, us to heavenly life. How do we share our 'emptying of self' experiences with the life of Jesus?

2. Jesus came to serve, not to be served

For *Lectio Divina*

Jesus called them to him and said, "You know that among the pagans the rulers lord it over them, and the great make their authority felt. This is not to happen among you. No; anyone who wants to be great among you must be your servant, and anyone who wants to be first among you must be your slave, just as the Son of Man came not to be served but to serve, and to give his life as a ransom for many."

Matthew 20:24-28

Themes

Pagan lording
Authority felt
Servant and slave
Being first
Jesus serving

Explanation

Pagan lording: Jesus considers that any overbearing exercise of authority – authoritarianism - is pagan, not something for people of the covenant.

Authority felt: Jesus considers the effect of such authoritarianism on people who are subject to such authority, their oppression.

Servant and slave: servants wait on those in charge; slaves are possessions, completely controlled by their owners.

Being first: the Twelve had been squabbling about places in God's kingdom after the mother of James and John asked for places at Jesus' right and left in the kingdom of God. Their squabbling was pagan.

Jesus serving: Jesus holds up to the Twelve the image, not merely of the servant waiting on authorities, but the service of a slave, even to the laying down of his life for others.

Voice

This text is from Matthew's Gospel, a Gospel of sermons, a Gospel of instruction, Jesus is laying down his law. Incidents in Jesus' life often form a basis for his instruction.

Other voices

The saying of Jesus occurs also in Luke 22:24-27, but, in another context, that of the Last Supper when the apostles are asking one another who could be the traitor. There are different nuances, for instance those who have authority are given the title Benefactor – and this is not to happen with them.

Jesus

Jesus recommends that the greatest must act as if they were the youngest. It finishes with Jesus saying, "Yet here I am among you as one who serves!" The passage in Mark 10:35-45 is the same as that in Matthew. Jesus shows the reality of serving in the washing of the feet at the Last Supper (John 13).

Deepening the meaning

1. The context of this saying of Jesus is the request of the mother of the sons of Zebedee, asking Jesus to promise positions of power for her sons in the kingdom. Jesus rebukes her, telling her that she does know what she is talking about and that discipleship will require her sons sharing in his suffering. They declare that they can – but Jesus says allotting places in the kingdom is the prerogative of God. How is this a key passage for understanding Jesus' ministry and service?

2. The Twelve had been following Jesus for a considerable time but still did not understand so much of what he was telling them, caught up in themselves and their own desires as they argue with one another about their importance. How do we get caught up in ourselves and our own desires, preventing our more authentic commitment to service?

3. How does Jesus make a contrast between what he has been teaching them about the kingdom of God and the "worldly" approach to authority and authoritarianism?

4. In many passages, Jesus had made a comment about those who thought they were the greatest, for instance taking the highest places at table and having to move down. Now he urges them not to think about themselves and their position but rather to think of

others. Are we sometimes seekers of the higher places at table or other situations?

5. How does Jesus offer himself as the example, the leader who is a servant, and not only a servant, but a slave giving himself completely in service to others, especially in his death as their ransom?

3. The Good Shepherd

For *Lectio Divina*

I am the good shepherd:
the good shepherd is one who lays down his life for his sheep.
The hired man, since he is not the shepherd
and the sheep do not belong to him,
abandons the sheep and runs away
as soon as he sees a wolf coming,
and then the wolf attacks and scatters the sheep;
this is because he is only a hired man
and has no concern for the sheep.
I am the good shepherd;
I know my own
and my own know me,
just as the Father knows me
and I know the Father;
and I lay down my life for my sheep.
And there are other sheep I have
that are not of this fold,
and these I have to lead as well.
They too will listen to my voice
and there will be only one flock,
and one shepherd.

John 10:11-16

Themes

I am
Shepherd
Sheep
Hireling
One flock, one Shepherd

Explanation

I am: whenever "I am" appears in John's Gospel, it is a reminder that Jesus is the Son of the Father, one with the Father. God had said to

Moses (Exodus 3:8) that he was the living God, "I am". Each reference in John's Gospel to "I am" indicates a different facet of Jesus himself as one with the Father.

Shepherd: before his selection by Samuel to be king, David was a shepherd. The image of shepherd belongs to the kings, not as absolute monarchs, but as servants of God. When they failed in their leadership, denounced by the prophets likes Jeremiah, it became clear that God was the true shepherd.

Sheep: flocks in Israel were small and precious, even to a stray sheep, an image which Jesus uses as an illustration to show God's love for every sheep, even those who are lost, rejoicing when they are found.

Hireling: the shepherd who merely did his work for pay, with little knowledge of the sheep, and careless in saving them from predators.

One flock, one shepherd: John's Gospel was written at the end of the first century. This sentiment reflects the experience of the early church and the desire for unity, calling back people who strayed, making converts, to form a Christian community.

Voice

This chapter on leadership, uses the image of the shepherd, applying to Jesus the image of "my shepherd is the Lord". The theology of John's Gospel is a reflection starting with his divinity and a moving down to humanity, Jesus one with the Father, who reveals the Father in many different ways – as in this true shepherd image.

Other voices

One can trace the shepherd imagery from the Second Book of Samuel where David is chosen to become king while he is working as a shepherd. By the time of the prophets, especially Jeremiah 23, the kings have failed in their leadership and have become bad shepherds, to be rejected. As in Psalm 23, the people recognise that God himself is the true shepherd. This is true of Isaiah 40, the book of Consolation, where God is described as a warrior with trophies but then suddenly is explained as a good shepherd, tender with his sheep. The main chapter of the Old Testament is Ezekiel 34. This is highlighted in the parables in Matthew and Luke with the shepherd searching for the lost sheep and rejoicing when it is found.

Jesus

Jesus is the good shepherd.

Deepening the meaning

1. The flocks of sheep in Israel were small, the shepherd knowing each of the sheep individually, keeping them safe, knowing them by name, searching for them when they were lost. How does this image of the sheep for the followers of Jesus highlight how precious each disciple is?
2. In the dangers where predators like bandits could attack, the shepherd not only protects the sheep but is ready to lay down his life for them, to save them. Looking back over the history of the church and at our own times of leadership and persecution, do we see shepherd-leaders?
3. The image of the good shepherd was taken up in the early church, for instance the image is applied to the elders in 1 Peter, and with statues, paintings, hymns and prayers. Why has it remained as one of the most vivid images of Jesus, and has entered into the language and the expectation of church leaders to the 'shepherds of the flock'.
4. It is good to explore chapter 34 of the prophet Ezekiel, in which so many of the images of shepherd and sheep find their origins and were drawn on for the gospel stories. Given different farming and agricultural developments, how apt are these images?
5. Since the Reformation, and the division of the churches, the language of a flock being one, one flock, one shepherd, has become a key aspiration of the ecumenical movement. Where do we stand today on these ecumenical aspirations?

4. A new commandment

For *Lectio Divina*

When he had washed their feet and put on his clothes again he went back to the table. "Do you understand" he said "what I have done to you? You call me Master and Lord, and rightly; so I am. If I, then, the Lord and Master, have washed your feet, you should wash each other's feet. I have given you an example so that you may copy what I have done to you.

John 13:13-15

Themes

Washing feet
Jesus, Master and Lord
Washing other's feet
Example
Copy

Explanation

Wash feet: in dusty Israel, it was a courtesy for guests to have their feet washed.

Jesus, Master and Lord: this is the beginning of the hour which will culminate in Jesus' death and resurrection. In this symbolic action, he emphasises his relationship with the Twelve.

Washing other's feet: this is the role of the servant who washes the feet of the guests.

Example: Jesus does a prophetic symbolic action which the Twelve can see and understand.

Copy: this is what the Twelve must do because of Jesus; no servant is greater than their master.

Voice

Once again, the Gospel of John, but part of the Last Supper narrative, marking the beginning of Jesus' hour in passing from this world to the next.

Other voices

In Matthew's Gospel, chapter 23, when Jesus denounces the double standards of the scribes and Pharisees, he once again refers to who is Master - and that is God, Jesus' Father. It is something of the same message that we find in the narrative of the washing of the feet. It takes us back to the servant songs, especially the third in Isaiah 50 and the fourth in Isaiah 52-53. The best-known gospel story of the washing of the feet is in Luke 7:36-50, where the sinful woman washes Jesus feet with her tears and anoints his feet with ointment, showing up the lack of courtesy and respect for Jesus from Simon, the host, who did not wash Jesus' feet, as common courtesy demanded.

Jesus

Jesus gives this new command: that leadership implies loving one another – as Jesus loved his disciples. In John 15:3, Jesus explains that this kind of loving leadership means laying down one's life for friends. He did it in death. We do it day by day in our lives.

Deepening the meaning

1. John tells the story of the washing of the feet in the context of the Last Supper. He does not have the story of the institution of the Eucharist, covered fully in the synoptic gospels and in 1 Corinthians 11. He puts the story at the beginning of Jesus' hour, of passing from this world to the next via his passion and death. How well do we combine in our imaginations all these aspects of the Last Supper?
2. While washing of feet is menial - the work of a servant - how does Jesus take it on as a symbol of leadership, extending courtesy, honouring those whose feet are washed, an example of Jesus not wanting to be served, but to serve?
3. Jesus is at pains to make clear the meaning of what he has done. He reminds them that he is Lord and Master – and he is. But washing feet and other services are what masters should do. How does Jesus break through expectations about the roles of masters and servants?
4. After the symbolic washing, Jesus emphasises that it is a symbol of the new law which he commands. How should we love each other,

but not just a mere loving, so to speak, but loving in the way that Jesus loved his disciples?

5. Just as the Old Covenant had its particular law, the Decalogue, so in this symbolic supper and washing of the feet, Jesus, the New Covenant, gives the New Covenant Law. How well do we understand Jesus as the fulfilment of God's revelation?

5. Authentic authority

For *Lectio Divina*

The scribes and the Pharisees occupy the chair of Moses. You must therefore do what they tell you and listen to what they say; but do not be guided by what they do: since they do not practise what they preach. They tie up heavy burdens and lay them on people's shoulders, but will they lift a finger to move them? Not they! Everything they do is done to attract attention, like wearing broader phylacteries and longer tassels, like wanting to take the place of honour at banquets and the front seats in the synagogues, being greeted obsequiously in the market squares and having people call them Rabbi.

You, however, must not allow yourselves to be called Rabbi, since you have only one Master, and you are all brothers. You must call no one on earth your father, since you have only one Father, and he is in heaven. Nor must you allow yourselves to be called teachers, for you have only one Teacher, the Christ. The greatest among you must be your servant. Anyone who exalts themself will be humbled and anyone who humbles himself will be exalted.

Matthew 23:1-12

Themes

Scribes and Pharisees
Obeying authorities
Double standards
Authentic authority
Being humbled and being exalted

Explanation

Scribes and Pharisees: the prominent religious leaders and interpreters of the Torah.

Obeying orders: Jesus is always very careful in advising others to work within the law (but sometimes running the risk of the authorities thinking he was not obeying the law).

Double standards: this is the strongest passage against the double standards of religious authorities, but criticisms by Jesus recur during the Gospels, for example the parable of the Pharisee and the tax-collector.

Authentic authority: authentic authority is God's law as expounded in the Scriptures and as interpreted with integrity by the authorities.

Being humbled and being exalted: Jesus often remarks that those who see themselves as above the law will find themselves humbled, and those who see themselves in a lowly light - according to the law - will be exalted.

Voice

This is Matthew's tone at its strongest: principled, logical and reasonable, acknowledging the hypocritical stances of so many of the religious leaders. And there are some strong metaphors to back this up.

Other voices

Jesus often incurs the criticism of scribes and Pharisees, concerning the nature of the law (and the consequent telling of the parable of the Good Samaritan), concerning his eating with tax collectors and prostitutes (giving the occasion for the telling of the parable of the Prodigal Son). When the authorities try to trap him, Jesus has an answer that bypasses their criticism, for example, with the woman taken in adultery, with paying taxes and rendering to Caesar what is Caesar's, and to God what is God's.

Jesus

The point with Jesus is that he is not a person of double standards, wants to take away no part of the law, will run risks in interpretation of the law (in healing the leper and touching him and, consequently, becoming leper himself for the time of quarantine).

Deepening the meaning

1. This is one of the strongest chapters in the Gospel, with Jesus' assertion of himself and his integrity, with critique of the double standards of the religious leaders of the time, the strongest passages where Jesus seems to be judging others. What was the initial impact of hearing these attacks by Jesus?

2. While there are metaphors in Matthew's Gospel, the images here are particularly telling, especially about tombs which look good on the outside but inside are the bones and corruption of the dead. What is Jesus' justification for this critique of the Pharisees?

3. In this condemnation of the leaders, there are many elements of Jesus' awareness of justice. He is also aware of proselytising and turning the converts into images of those converting. How relevant are Jesus' comments on some religious authorities today?

4. Jesus makes the appeal to Moses as the principal lawgiver of the old law, his authority and the people of Israel obeying these laws. What is the basis of true religious authority?

5. However, what is the important lesson from Jesus in this text concerning the respect due to the leaders in terms of doing what they say but the key issue of not putting into practice what they do?

3. THE INTEGRITY OF CREATION

1. Creation

For *Lectio Divina*

God created great sea-serpents and every kind of living creature with which the waters teem, and every kind of winged creature.... God blessed them, saying "Be fruitful, multiply, and fill the waters of the sea: and let the birds multiply upon the earth" ...
God made every kind of wild beast, every kind of cattle, and every kind of land reptile.
God said, "Let us make man in our own image, in the likeness of ourselves and let them be masters of the fish of the sea, the birds of heaven, the cattle, all the wild beasts and all the reptiles that crawl upon the earth'...
God blessed them, saying to them, "Be fruitful, multiply, fill the earth and conquer it. Be masters of the fish of the sea, the birds of heaven and all living animals on the earth. God said, "See, I give you all the seed-bearing plants that are upon the whole earth, and all the trees with seed-bearing fruit; this shall be your food. To all wild beasts, all birds of heaven and all living reptiles on the earth I give all the foliage of plants for food. And so it was. God saw all he had made and indeed it was very good...
Thus heaven and earth were completed with all their array.

Genesis 1:20 to 2:1

Themes

God created
Every kind of living creature
God created humankind
Mastering and conquering
Stewardship

Explanation

God created: the Old Testament vision that the world - humans, animals, plant-life, the land and the sea - all depend on God.

Every kind of living creature: while God speaks of some animals as food for humankind, there are many living creatures that exist within the framework of sea or land and its development.

God created humankind: along with the rest of the creation, humankind is seen as its peak, creation that could know and understand and respond to God.

Mastering and conquering: these are the words used in translations of Genesis in past times. The emphasis now would be on mastering in terms of stewardship.

Stewardship: the relationship between humankind and the rest of creation, not a simple mastering and conquering and using up all creation till it was exhausted, simply to support humankind. The Genesis passage indicates that humans are created in the image of God, who was a creator rather than a conqueror.

Voice

This passage comes from the prologue of Genesis, the chapters of pre-history, so to speak, placed as an introduction to the story of the patriarchs and the beginnings of the Hebrew people. These chapters were finally written later in Israel's history, gathering together the oral tradition, the influence of stories from neighbouring countries, and after the experience of the exile in Babylon. The chapters date from the fifth and fourth centuries BC.

Other voices

In Genesis 2, there is an alternate story of creation which focuses on Adam and Eve, the idyllic life in Eden, the temptation of the fruit of the tree of the knowledge of good and evil, the fall and Adam and Eve expelled from Eden, and to work the land with the sweat of their brow. Later in the Wisdom literature, there will be a new creation when the Spirit of God renews the face of the earth.

Jesus

Jesus does not have any explicit references to the stories of creation. his approach to nature is certainly not a conquering approach.

Deepening the meaning

1. How is the poetry, rather than the science, of the six days of creation and God's day of rest, a poetic presentation of the creative God in relationship to our world, its life, and humans – a spiritual and theological imagining of creation for the Hebrew people? For ourselves?
2. The emphasis is on creation by God's Spirit hovering over the initial chaos, God's Word being all-powerful, achieving what it says, on each day of creation. What does the poetry convey about God's power and the beauty of creation?
3. The Genesis emphasis is also on God's delight in looking at creation with the stressing of God seeing that it is all very good. How do we share in God's vision of seeing that all creation is very good?
4. The industrial revolution in the West, and the image of progress, led to many questions of how to interpret 'mastering and conquering creation' as meaning 'using it and consuming it to produce more and more for human consumption'. What does mastery of creation mean in terms of fostering all creation?
5. During the 20th century, and the discovery of vast resources, especially for energy, the mastering and conquering continued. However, a new consciousness arose, the idea of stewardship, managing God's creation well without exploiting it, consciousness of preserving the environment and what is called eco-theology. How well do we understand human stewardship of creation? And the merits of eco-theology?

2. Destruction and new creation

For *Lectio Divina*

God said to Noah, "The end has come for all things of flesh; I have decided this, because the earth is full of violence of man's making...
From all living creatures, from all flesh, you must take two of each kind aboard the ark, to save their lives with yours, they must be a male and a female. Of every kind of bird, of every kind of animal and of every kind of reptile on the ground, two must go with you so that their lives may be saved...
Then God said to Noah, "Come out of the ark, you yourself, your wife, your sons, and your sons' wives with you. As for all the animals with you, all things of flesh, whether the birds or animals or reptiles that crawl on the earth, bring them out with you. Let them swarm on the earth; let them be fruitful and multiply on the earth...

Genesis 6 to 8

Themes

Violence from humans' making
All living creatures
Two by two
Bring them out with you
Let them be fruitful and multiply on the earth

Explanation

Violence from human's making: the injunction from Genesis was that humans should be masters of the earth in the sense of exercising a stewardship; exploitation of creation by violent means negates God's injunction, brings on destruction for humankind.

All living creatures: in the creation story in Genesis, every living creature is considered good and its well-being should be fostered rather than destroyed by humankind.

Two by two: the flood is not the end of the world; it is described as a destructive punishment for human sinfulness and exploitation. Which means that, animals two by two, male and female, are to be saved for the re-population of all living creatures.

Bring them out with you: Noah is to be the steward for the replenishment of animal life in the new world.

Let them be fruitful and multiply on the earth: the re-creation of the life of living creatures on the earth is an image of creation and its fruitfulness.

Voice

The flood/deluge story of Genesis is a key narrative in the prologue to the history of Abraham and the patriarchs. It continues the story of creation, but highlights human sinfulness and the need for purging and cleansing. It takes the form of a flood story, a popular kind of narrative in the ancient near East, but the Hebrew tradition takes the key elements to illustrate God's relationship to human beings and to creation.

Other voices

The story of Noah and the flood is used in other parts of the Old and New Testaments, Jesus using it as an image for the end of the world; the Second Letter of Peter also uses it in this context. Noah himself is one of those ancestors praised in the book of Sirach 44:17-19: Noah was found perfectly virtuous; in the time of wrath he became the scion; because of him a remnant was preserved for the earth at the coming of the Flood. Everlasting covenants were made with him that never again should every living creature perish by flood.

Jesus

Jesus draws on the knowledge of his audience concerning the Flood and its meaning. He uses the references in an allegory for the end of the world, Matthew 24:37-41. Jesus highlights the selfishness and exploitation of people who have turned from God and are not ready for God's judgment.

Deepening the meaning

1. The story of the Flood is part of the Genesis creation and re-creation story in the consciousness of the Judeo-Christian tradition. It was shared by other cultures neighbouring that of Israel. For Israel, it is a story of human infidelity, exploitation and the consequences. What is the 'moral' of the Deluge story?

2. With the focus on the animals, how is this something of a new creation story, in which God creates living creatures with human beings to be the stewards of their life?
3. In a sense, Noah and his wife are a new Adam and Eve, who do not sin but enable creation to begin again and prosper. How does the Deluge story indicate God's continuing love and care for us rather than destroying us?
4. The Scriptures are constant in their stories of the care for creation. Why is this an obligation for human beings so that all creatures may multiply and prosper?
5. How does the Noah and flood story serve as an allegory for the contemporary ecological movement: for humans to repent of their exploitation, to avoid disaster, to be creative in their stewardship for all environments and creatures to flourish?

3. Praise of creation

For *Lectio Divina*

Every thing that grows on the earth! bless the Lord:
give glory and eternal praise to him.
Springs of water! bless the Lord:
give glory and eternal praise to him.
Seas and rivers! bless the Lord:
give glory and eternal praise to him.
Sea beasts and everything that lives in water! bless the Lord:
give glory and eternal praise to him.
Birds of heaven! All bless the Lord:
give glory and eternal praise to him.
Animals wild and tame! All bless the Lord:
give glory and eternal praise to him.

Daniel 3:76-82

Themes

Every thing that grows on the earth
Seas and rivers
Birds and animals
Bless the Lord
Glory and eternal praise

Explanation

Every thing that grows on the earth: throughout the Old Testament, things that grow on the earth are frequently named and specified, from the Genesis creation account to the images used by the prophets and from Jesus himself.

Seas and rivers: the beauty of water on earth and, by implication, the beauty of all the land.

Birds and animals: again, throughout the Old Testament, there are many references to specific birds and animals, the living creatures of God's creation.

Bless the Lord: blessing is wishing well to another, as well as an acknowledgment of sacredness which, in all of creation, leads to the praise of God.

Glory and eternal praise: this is a constant theme of hymns and Psalms throughout the Scriptures, the image that Gerard Manley Hopkins uses: The world is charged with the grandeur of God – which means that creation is a manifestation of God which reflects his glory, enabling human beings to praise God.

Voice

This Canticle comes from the book of Daniel. The book was written later in Israel's history, a morale-boosting collection of oracles and stories and, influenced by the Psalms.

Other voices

Starting with Psalm 148, this kind of praise of God for creation, in and through creation, is a common theme. It can be seen in Psalm 93. It can also be found in the book of Job, when God challenges the suffering man about his faith and his fate. Two full chapters of the wonder of creation can be found in chapters 38 and 39.

Jesus

As will be seen, Jesus, from Galilee, a fruitful area of Palestine compared with Samaria or Judaea, shows his appreciation of nature, in his parables and in his metaphors.

Deepening the meaning

1. When considering the integrity of creation, how do we appreciate that the Scriptures are full of nature, descriptions of nature in all its manifestations, and poetic use of nature in images?
2. This passage is in the form of a Canticle, and can be prayed as a hymn, even as a litany of God and nature. How contemporary is this canticle as well as its themes, and its praise of God?
3. There is a tradition in the Psalms of a category of "Praise Psalms". This hymn is one the most amplified, and the implication of praising God from nature is joy. Do we appreciate the spirituality of joy in nature?
4. God's contest with the suffering Job is resolved by appealing to his own appreciation of nature, its power and majesty, and therefore

the power and majesty of God. How do we share Job's submission in faith to the all-powerful God and creator and sustainer of nature?

5. From verse 82, with all the references to human beings, to priests, servants of the Lord, devout and humble hearted people, humanity forms part of this creation which gives glory and eternal praise to God. How can we foster this in our own lives and the lives of others?

4. Jesus and nature

For *Lectio Divina*

Surely life means more than food, and the body more than clothing! Look at the birds in the sky. They do not sow or reap or gather into barns; yet your heavenly Father feeds them. Are you not worth much more than they are? Can any of you, for all their worrying, add one single cubit to their span of life? And why worry about clothing? Think of the flowers growing in the field; they never have to work or spin; yet I assure you that not even Solomon in all his regalia was robed like one of these. Now if that is how God clothes the grass in the field which is there today and thrown into the furnace tomorrow, will he not much more look after you, you of little faith?

Matthew 6:25-30

Themes

Human worry and concern
Providence
Flowers and glory
Beauty just in being there
God's care of nature and of humankind

Explanation

Human worry and concern: the Gospel acknowledges food and clothing as necessities for human beings – but life is far more than that. We can worry but it does not mean that we can extend our lives at all.

Providence: God's continued care of all creation, of every human, and, as the Gospel reminds us, birds are not busy about many things and God feeds them.

Flowers and glory: the Gospel reminds us that the natural beauty of the flowers is more splendid than Solomon in his regal robes.

Beauty just in being there: flowers do not have to sow, they do not spin, they are simply there. They are just beautiful in themselves and being there to be admired by people, even though they will soon die.

God's care of nature and humankind: providence extends to the simple creatures, the birds, the flowers in the field, which lead short lives. We must draw the conclusion that God cares for nature and, of course, for his human creation.

Voice

This passage comes from the Sermon on the Mount, between sayings about being slaves to God or money, and of warnings not to judge or we will be judged. It is a lyrical interlude – poetic - in the middle of Jesus' preaching, with a strong message about providence – but with the appeal to the beauty of nature which God sustains.

Other voices

This passage is also in Luke 12:22-31 where there is an emphasis on humans not worrying; both Gospels indicate that it is the pagans of this world who set their hearts on all these things. There are many passages in the Old Testament, hymns about nature, for instance in Isaiah 35:1-10, where a wilderness will blossom with flowers and the wastelands will rejoice and bloom. This growth of nature is linked with God's healing powers to make humans whole.

Jesus

This is Jesus himself using nature images to communicate his message about God's care, God's Providence, that birds and flowers are to be appreciated and that the meanings of our lives are to be understood through their beauty, just being there. This is part of the stewardship of humans over nature. Jesus himself uses nature in some of his parables, especially that of the sower and the wheat, and that of the weeds in the fields, images of the mustard seed.

Deepening the meaning

1. How could this passage from the Sermon on the Mount be used for a liturgy, for a Eucharistic celebration of the integrity of creation, the harmony between humans and nature, which Jesus himself acknowledges?
2. There is a message here for those who want to control the land and want to control animals, birds, fish… How do we appreciate that all creation is alive, has its beauty, and humans need to contribute to sustaining that?

3. Human concern and, especially, worry, come easily to people, especially in their 'struggles' with the seasons and the forces of nature. How do we contribute to the great challenge to find harmonious ways of dealing with seasons and nature?
4. Humans are very often concerned about employment, industry, the means for making a living, and rightly so. How do we respond to the challenge that these concerns are fulfilled in harmony with nature?
5. For recent decades, the concern for the environment has almost become a faith for many people. The Scriptures highlight how they are in harmony with contemporary aspirations for eco-philosophy and eco-theology. How can we share this faith with non-believers in God who believe in nature?

5. Creation and Eucharist

For *Lectio Divina*

When the hour came he took his place at table, and the apostles with him. And he said to them, "I have longed to eat this Passover with you before I suffer because, I tell you, I shall not eat it again until it is fulfilled in the kingdom of God".
Then taking a cup, he gave thanks and said, "Take this and share it among you, because from now on, I tell you, I shall not drink wine until the kingdom of God comes".
Then, he took some bread, and when he had given thanks, broke it and gave it to them, saying, "This is my body which will be given for you; do this as a memorial of me". He did the same with the cup after supper, and said, "This cup is the new covenant in my blood which will be poured out for you'.

Luke 22:14-20

Themes

Passover
Covenant
Bread and wine
Creation filled with divine presence
Eucharist and Memorial

Explanation

Passover: for the Jews of Jesus' time, the celebration of the liberation from Egypt, the Covenant with its law and ritual, the memorial of God's graciousness in the life of the Hebrew people. The actions which Jesus does at this celebration are most solemn, a new liberation, New Covenant with new law and with new ritual.

Covenant: the pledge that God would be faithful to the people no matter what they did. Now a new pledge of God's fidelity in Jesus.

Bread and wine: as the liturgy says at the offertory, 'fruit of the earth and work of human hands'. This is offering the staple food, bread, and the drink that delights, according to the Psalms, the human heart, wine.

Creation filled with divine presence: symbolically and sacramentally, the basic bread and wine of ordinary creation can be filled with God's presence.

Eucharist and Memorial: since the Eucharist is the core worship of the church, and since it brings to mind what Jesus did on the night of the Last Supper as well as what he did on Calvary, the ordinariness of creation is at the centre of Eucharist, showing us how creation is consecrated and blessed. God is present in creation and it has always been good. Now Jesus has made nature sacramental in the Eucharist.

Voice

The three synoptic Gospels have similar narratives of the Last Supper and of the 'institution' of the Eucharist. This is a core experience for the church which becomes part of the great tradition which Paul already speaks of in 1 Corinthians 11.

Other voices

The four Gospels have Last Supper narratives, the Synoptics focusing on the Eucharist itself, John focusing on the washing of the feet at the special "hour" for God to be glorified, and through the example of the washing of the feet, giving the new covenant law: loving one another as Jesus has loved us, laying down his life for friends.

Jesus

It is Jesus who takes the bread and who takes the wine and, like an Old Testament prophet holding them out, declares that they are his body and blood, the pledge of the new covenant which will be fulfilled on Calvary. With the bread and the wine, Jesus and nature are one.

Deepening the meaning

1. The Passover was the key celebration for the Hebrew people and, therefore, for Jesus. It takes up the major themes of the Old Testament, escape from Egypt and being spared, the desert experience, the covenant at Mt Sinai, the new law and the ratification of the covenant in ritual. The celebration developed over the centuries, incorporating the theme of the lamb as the victim to be slain, the Holocaust as well as the Communion sacrifice. Does this help us appreciate our celebration of the Eucharist?

2. There is an emotional factor in Luke's telling of the story, the long time that Jesus says he has been longing for the Last Supper before he died. The apostles are highlighted as the main people at the supper. Do we keep well this memorial and pass on the tradition within the Christian communities?
3. Jesus has said that he is the bread of life, and now he makes it sacramentally real for his disciples, for them to share. And it is the wine, signalled at the wedding feast at Cana, where life-giving water becomes Jesus' wine. What is our appreciation of this real presence of Jesus?
4. This is the memorial of Jesus laying down his life us, but also of his new rising to life. How do we appreciate this in our Communion?
5. In recent decades, theologians and spiritual writers, reflecting on the nature and the environment, have indicated that the Eucharist, bread and wine blessed and shared, is a powerful symbol of the integrity of creation. How do we understand this?

4. THE HEART OF GOD

1. God sets his heart on us

For *Lectio Divina*

If the Lord set his heart on you and chose you, it was not because you out-numbered other peoples: you were the least of all peoples. It was for love of you and to keep the oath he swore to your ancestors that the Lord brought you out with his mighty hand and redeemed you from the house of slavery... Know then that the Lord your God is God indeed, the faithful God who is true to his covenant and his graciousness for a thousand generations towards those who love him and keep his commandments...

Deuteronomy 7:7-9

Themes

Heart
Redeemed
Covenant
Faithful
Graciousness

Explanation

Heart: the language of heart is a result of the interventions of the prophets who 'personalised' the religious attitudes and behaviour of the people, introducing the heart as the centre of the people's faith. Deuteronomy begins to speak of the heart of God.

Redeemed: the people were indebted to the Lord for bringing them out of Egypt, saving them, but also forgiving them their infidelity and sinfulness.

Covenant: the core of Old Testament religion, the pledge by the Lord to be faithful to the chosen people, reaching out to them even when they turned away.

Faithful: God being true to the very divine self, having given the pledge of covenant, there was no turning back for God who must always reach out to the people, no matter what they do.

Graciousness: the quality of the lovingkindness of the covenant which then described the action of God and of God's heart.

Voice

While the book of Deuteronomy is a book of the Pentateuch, its chapters were, in fact, written down before the other books of the Torah, in the last century before the fall of Jerusalem, the 7th century BC, when the priests and elders rethought the covenant stories and wrote their reflections in the book of Deuteronomy.

Other voices

It is in the Psalms that there are descriptions of God's love, mercy, forgiveness, and the language of the heart.

Jesus

Jesus will draw on this language of the heart in describing himself as gentle and humble in heart, like the God of the covenant. On the cross, Jesus' side will be pierced and blood and water flow from it, the complete outpouring from his heart.

Deepening the meaning

1. There had been a language of God's choice of his people, often expressed in imagery, with some gentleness, as in Exodus 19 where God describes carrying the chosen people on eagle's wings, setting them apart because all the world was God's and God could choose favourites from this equality. Do we appreciate these images of God's ever-tender love for us?
2. The prophets would use the language of a new heart. The hardened heart of stone would be taken out of the people and replaced by heart of flesh, through which they would know and love the Lord, rather than being taught about this love (Jeremiah 31:31-34). Have we experienced times when our hearts were hard but a spiritual experience has turned them into loving hearts of flesh?
3. While the Hebrew people considered that life was in the blood, the heart was at the very core of a human being, on which the covenant law could be written. How do we understand a 'spirituality of the heart'?

4. The result of the Lord's knowing his people and their knowing him is not just an intellectual knowledge, of the mind. The Hebrew implies both knowing and loving. How are we and all people to know and love God because of the Lord's heart-choice of them?

5. The fidelity of God means that there is to be no ending of this choice, this covenant, and this covenant love. Do we believe in God's never-ending, never-failing love?

2. Nearest to the Father's heart

For *Lectio Divina*

Indeed, from his fullness we have, all of us, received –
yes, grace in return for grace,
since, though the Law was given through Moses,
grace and truth have come through Jesus Christ...
No one has ever seen God;
it is the only Son, who is nearest to the Father's heart,
who has made him known.

John 1:16-18

Themes

The fullness of God
Grace
Truth
The Son's revelation of the Father
The Father's heart

Explanation

The fullness of God: as the Old Testament developed, the theme of abundance of God's graciousness was developed by the prophets, the writers of the Psalms and in the Wisdom literature. Amongst other graces, this means giving sight to the blind, hearing to the deaf, the lame walking... And freedom from all kinds of imprisonment.

Grace: Grace embodies God's graciousness and love, spontaneous gifting of his people, at special times, which became part of theological language about God's dealing with us.

Truth: an important theme for John's Gospel and John's letters: what is truth? Truth is integrity.

The Son's revelation of the Father: These verses are the conclusion of the prologue to John's Gospel: the Word was with God, and the Word was God, and the Word was made flesh, the Son revealing the Father.

The Father's heart: the verse indicates the intimacy between the Father and the Son. This is language about God's innermost being, heart.

Voice

John's Gospel came together at the end of the first century, drawing on the other Gospels which had been in circulation for decades. This is the story of Jesus, presuming on his union with the Father, his divinity, and highlighting this.

Other voices

The themes from this passage are echoed right throughout the Gospel, when Jesus is the Way, the Truth and the Life. It echoes through the different stories of John's Gospel, Jesus acting from the heart, showing the heart of the Father, towards the woman at the well, to the man born blind, to Lazarus. The themes also appear in the first letter of John.

Jesus

The union of Jesus with the Father is repeated throughout John's Gospel, especially in chapter 6 when Jesus says that no one comes to the Father except through him. At the Last Supper and at various other occasions, Jesus gives the Father thanks and says that the Father will be glorified in him. Although suffering, Jesus is seen on the cross as manifesting the glory of the Father.

Deepening the meaning

1. The language of John 1 seems to be that of a hymn of the early church, naming the Son as the Word of God, with God, who was God, through whom everything was created, so that light would shine in the darkness. How do we appreciate Jesus as the Revelation of the Father?
2. 'From his fullness we have all received.' How do we as humans, as created, have life from the Father, sharing in the fullness of life with the Son?
3. The Old Covenant on Sinai was mediated through Moses. Jesus is the new covenant. At the Last Supper, Jesus gave a new law: to love as he loved. What does it meant that the qualities of the new covenant are not described in the language of law, but of grace and truth?

4. Jesus is the image of the invisible God in our world, the Word made flesh, making God known through word and image. What does it mean that in looking at what Jesus did and listening to what he said that we actually see and hear God?

5. The Gospel has the language of God's heart, and it is in the heart of Jesus, the human heart, that divine love could be present in our world. How is the divine love of the Father shown in the love of the human heart of Jesus?

3. God's gentleness of heart

For *Lectio Divina*

Everything has been entrusted to me by my Father; and no one knows the Son except the Father, just as no one knows the Father except the Son and those to whom the Son choose to reveal him.

Come to me, all you labour and our overburdened, and I will give you rest. Shoulder my yoke and learn from me, for I am gentle and humble in heart, and you will find rest of your souls. Yes, my yoke is easy and my burden light.

Matthew 11:27-30

Themes

Knowing the Father
Everything entrusted to Jesus
Shoulder my yoke
Gentle and humble in heart
Rest for your souls

Explanation

Knowing the Father: in this passage, Jesus considers knowing and loving the Father as one of his delights, blessing the Father that this can be revealed to those who are simple of heart, like children.

Everything entrusted to Jesus: this is a prayer of joy from Jesus, expressing in human terms how the Father has loved him and given this revelation to him.

Shoulder my yoke: Jesus had shouldered the yoke of becoming one with us and invites us to share this experience with him, sharing in his ministry.

Gentle and humble in heart: echoes of the beatitudes, the gentle inheriting the earth, the humble being the truly in poor in spirit – as Jesus was.

Rest for your souls: an image from the prophets, especially in Zephaniah 3, that, ultimately, those who remained faithful, the poor of the earth and the gentle, will be led to places of peace.

Voice

The Synoptic Gospels were written down in the middle and latter part of the first century. They gathered together memories of Jesus' sayings and deeds. They assemble them in thematic ways, for instance the prayer of Jesus and his joy is linked with his invitation to share his ministry and to share the rewards of rest.

Other voices

This prayer of Jesus glorifying his Father is found also in Luke's Gospel, in the context of his disciples having gone out on ministry and returning, rejoicing. Jesus gives the glory for all of this to the Father. The descriptions of people as needing rest and Jesus as gentle and humble echoes the prophets as well as the expressions of the beatitudes.

Jesus

In John's Gospel, Jesus frequently gives glory to the Father and sees in what he says and does the glorifying of the Father. Versions of the beatitudes are found in Matthew 5 and in Luke 6.

Deepening the meaning

1. Jesus says that everything has been entrusted to him by his Father, including the love and intimacy of the very heart of the Father. What does this reveal of the full humanity of Jesus?
2. The implication of no revelation to the learned and the clever is that there is too much reliance on the human mind and its workings. Do we understand the openness and simplicity of children who are able to accept what is revealed to them rather than critically analysing what is offered?
3. With Jesus offering this invitation to his followers, especially those who experience hardship and oppression, he is manifesting the love in his own heart. How is this a manifestation of the love in God's heart?
4. Matthew's Gospel can sound very stern at times, straightforward narrative, no-frills parable telling, many sermons and injunctions, the fulfilment of the old law. But this is Jesus sounding like the prophets and their personal calls to following their message. How do we hear the different tones of Jesus in the different Gospels?

5. Burdens must be carried but how does sharing the experience with Jesus mean that the load is lighter, more manageable (just as oxen ploughing the field are yoked together to give them a sense of direction so that the field may be ploughed)?

4. The heart of the law

For *Lectio Divina*

There was a lawyer who, to disconcert Jesus, stood up and said to him, "Master, what must I do to inherit eternal life?" He said to him, "What is written in the Law? What do you read there?" He replied, "You must love the Lord your God with all your heart, with all your soul, with all your strength, and with all your mind, and your neighbour as yourself". "You have answered right," said Jesus "do this and life is yours." But the man was anxious to justify himself and said to Jesus, "And who is my neighbour?"

Luke 10:25-29

Themes

Disconcerting Jesus
The commandments
The heart of the law
The second commandment
Who is my neighbour?

Explanation

Disconcerting Jesus: this is a key passage of Luke's Gospel, and it is given a special setting: an interpreter of the religious law wants to upset Jesus, to trick him, and not only asks him about the law and eternal life, but in pique at Jesus' provocation about love of neighbour, retorts with one of the key questions of the gospel.

The commandments: love of God is at the core of the Decalogue and the other commandments of Scripture. The Shema – 'Listen O Israel' (Deuteronomy 6:4) is the key profession of faith in God's law, continuing to the present day.

The heart of the law: Deuteronomy 6:4 refers to the depth of commitment to God's law, not only of soul and strength and mind, but with heart. And it is Deuteronomy which highlighted God's own heart reaching out to those who obeyed the law.

The second commandment: love of neighbour, as oneself, comes from Torah texts, like Leviticus 19:18.

Who is my neighbour?: with the story of the Good Samaritan, we understand that those who were despised, beneath recognition, condemned as enemies were, according to the law, neighbours who merited God's love and compassion.

Voice

The voice is that of the Lukan community, and the Gospel is not only for Jews but for Gentiles, for everyone, something which is seen in the upholding of the hospitable Samaritan as an image of God, of God's compassionate love for someone who has been brutalised, a victim and in need.

Voices

The original story which Jesus draws on in telling the parable of the Good Samaritan can be found in 2 Chronicles 28:15, part of the narrative of Israel's history. It speaks of a battle and Jericho and people putting wounded men on donkeys and returning them to Samaria. The sentiment of the parable is dramatised in Paul's hymn to love and charity, 1 Corinthians 13.

Jesus

Two examples of Jesus and his neighbourliness to Samaritans are his encounter with the woman at the well in John 4 and his welcoming of the leper, the only one out of the ten who returned to thank Jesus for his healing – and he was a Samaritan (Luke 17:11-19). In Matthew's Gospel, Jesus goes beyond the boundaries of Israel and grants the wish of the Syro-Phoenician woman (Matthew 15:21-28) and was noted as moving around the territory on the far side of the Sea of Galilee, healing people, including the man possessed by a devil. He also healed the servant of the Roman Centurion.

Deepening the meaning

1. Jesus experienced some difficulties with religious leaders who were absorbed in interpretations of the law, mental exercises about the law, rather than examining their consciences about how they put it into practice. The lawyer was an interpreter of the law and his petulance towards Jesus led him to ask one of the most important of gospel questions. Do we appreciate the interconnection between love of God and love of neighbour?

2. One of the things to notice about Jesus is that he is a teacher who does not always give answers but answers a question with a challenging question. What are the questions that God is asking of us now?
3. Jesus is an upholder of the law, knows the Scriptures and their meanings, even though his critics often try to trap him in his interpretations of scriptural passages, as with the condemnation of the woman taken in adultery (John 8). How does Jesus go beyond (and go deeper than) the letter of the law?
4. While Jesus did not travel extensively (that was to come later with Paul, Peter and the other Apostles), he was conscious of those from other territories. The good news was not exclusive to Israel. And how is the Good News not exclusive to us as Jesus' followers?
5. The language that the parable uses about the Samaritan - moved with compassion, bandaging wounds and pouring oil and wine on them, caring afterwards for the wounded man - reflect words and phrases that are used about God, like the words of the father in the parable of the prodigal son (Luke 15). How is the Good Samaritan an image of the loving Father, of compassion and care in the heart of God?

5. The fullness of God

For *Lectio Divina*

Out of his infinite glory, may he give you the power through his Spirit for your hidden self to grow strong, so that Christ may live in your hearts through faith, and then, planted in love and built on love, you will with all the saints have strength to grasp the breadth and the length, the height and the depth; until knowing the love of Christ, which is beyond all knowledge, you are filled with the utter fullness of God.

Ephesians 3:16-19.

Themes

Hidden self
Live in your hearts
The love of Christ beyond all knowledge
Built on love
The utter fullness of God

Explanation

Hidden self: the inner core, the heart of every human being, capable of being filled with grace in order fully to love God.

Live in your hearts: the interior life of faith and grace that Paul continually urges his readers to acknowledge and to grow into.

The love of Christ beyond all knowledge: this is the love for Jesus which is planted in love and built on love, shared with all the saints, those called to this discipleship, which enables the disciple to receive the love of Jesus which, of themselves, they could never attain.

Built on love: this love is the gift of Jesus when we are empowered by the Spirit, that leads to a love of the Father.

The utter fullness of God: this is the mystery of God, the absolute gift of love and loving kindness, that we could not comprehend of ourselves, but it is the gift of being completely filled with God's love and presence.

Voice

The Letter to the Ephesians is considered by scholars not to have been written directly by Paul himself but by his disciples, who had lived and worked with him, listened to him, read his words, and so were capable of distilling much of his thought and inspiration into this letter.

Other voices

Other letters of Paul, most notably the Letter to the Romans and those to the Corinthians, as well as the final messages at the end of Paul's life in the Letter to the Philippians, are filled with this theme of the utter fullness of God. This theme is expressed in different language in the first Letter of John, the hymn in the opening verses of our sharing the experience of living with Jesus as a human being as well as the promise of seeing God as God really is (1 John 3:2). The other classic chapter on love from Paul is 1 Corinthians 13.

Jesus

Jesus prays in this way to the Father in Matthew 11:25-27 and Luke 10:21-22.

Deepening the meaning

1. This passage is introduced as being a prayer of Paul, kneeling before the Father, proclaiming that it is the Father from whom every family, whether spiritual or natural, takes its name. How well does this passage sum up our image of God?
2. The gift of the utter fullness of God comes from what Paul calls God's infinite glory, a poetic word of admiration and praise as well as awe of God. This is Pauline language – what words and phrases are we most at home with in speaking about God?
3. This passage focuses on the interior life, not only of faith and commitment, but of hope and of that virtue of love which Paul says is the greatest. Do we have words when we are asked to speak about our interior life?
4. Paul uses the image of measurements, not for hyperbole, but in order to communicate the infinite dimensions, so to speak, of the fullness of God's love. How close is God to us? Is God distant?

5. Our being invited to share in the love of Jesus means that we are invited into the very life and love of God's heart. There is a wonderful phrase, At Home with God. Are we?

www.ingramcontent.com/pod-product-compliance
Lightning Source LLC
Chambersburg PA
CBHW051948290426
44110CB00015B/2157